Charles Butler

Our treaty with Spain

Triumphant diplomacy

Charles Butler

Our treaty with Spain
Triumphant diplomacy

ISBN/EAN: 9783337231972

Printed in Europe, USA, Canada, Australia, Japan

Cover: Foto ©ninafisch / pixelio.de

More available books at **www.hansebooks.com**

OUR

TREATY WITH SPAIN

TRIUMPHANT DIPLOMACY

ANNOTATED BY

CHARLES HENRY BUTLER

WASHINGTON LAW BOOK COMPANY
1422 F St., N. W.
WASHINGTON, D. C.
1898

OUR TREATY WITH SPAIN.

TRIUMPHANT DIPLOMACY.

The event for which the country has been waiting with the keenest expectancy and impatience has at last transpired. The Treaty of Peace by which the war with Spain, temporarily ended by the Protocol of August 12th, has been finally terminated, peace restored to the two countries, and freedom and liberty assured to those whom this country was bound to, and did, protect, has been concluded and exchanged by the High Commissioners representing the two sovereign nations engaged in the struggle.

All that now remains to make the treaty the supreme law of the land is for the President to transmit it for ratification to the Senate of the United States, in accordance with those provisions of the Constitution which clothe the President with "power, by and with the advice and consent of the Senate, to make treaties, provided two-thirds of the Senators present concur," and which also provide that "all treaties which shall be made under the authority of the United States shall be the supreme law of the land," and for the Senate to formally ratify it.

The High Commissioners of the United States will, on their arrival at the end of this week, deliver the original executed copy of the treaty to the President, and thereupon will be relieved from further duties as Commissioners, although three of them will, in their capacity as Senators, have the further duty of voting for the ratification, by the body of which they are such distinguished members, of the fruit of their labors.

While the exact text of the treaty may, pending its ratification and pursuant to custom, remain officially undisclosed, the fact that it has already been published in Spanish newspapers has made its contents an open secret, for there is no apparent reason to doubt the general accuracy of the text which was obtained and published through the enterprise of the newspapers.

This annotation of the treaty, therefore, is published on the assumption that the "Sun" text is correct, and, as it will be impossible to obtain any official copy of the treaty until it shall have been published, either by direction of the President or the Senate, this text is the only one available at the present time.

Some discrepancies will undoubtedly appear, as, according to press accounts, the text published was an independent translation of the Spanish version of the treaty. Such discrepancies, however, will probably not materially affect the general description of the concessions made in, and the principles established by, the treaty.

The negotiation of this treaty is a triumph of American diplomacy, or, to use a more proper expression, let us say, of American statesmanship, and the President and the High Commissioners who represented the country are to be congratulated upon the success of the final struggle of the war.

As great a victory has been won as when Commodore, now Admiral, Dewey destroyed the entire Spanish fleet in Cavité Bay with the indirect loss of only two men; as when Admirals Sampson and Schley and the commanders of the vessels in the squadron off Santiago sank Cevera's fleet with the loss of only one man; as when Santiago, and thereby, eventually, the whole of Cuba, was captured with a loss of less than ten per cent of the corresponding loss in the Civil War, when the number of men engaged, and the time consumed, in the conflict are considered.

In the case of the treaty, as in the victories of our naval and military heroes, everything has been gained for the United States and nothing has been lost or surrendered, nor have any indefinite obligations been assumed, or liabilities created, except in so far as the United States have very properly agreed to judge and settle the claims of their own citizens for such losses as they have innocently incurred through Spanish misrule in Cuba.

Let them say what they will about the necessity of special education for our diplomats, there are no greater schools of diplomacy in the world than the Department of State, and the Committees on Foreign Relations and Foreign Affairs in the two Houses of Congress, and in the present instance, all the members of the Commission, as well as every one associated with them, have taken the full course in practical diplomacy, either in the Department, one or both of those Committees, or in active diplomatic service, and the treaty gives evidence of the thoroughness of their education; throughout all the negotiations there has also been felt the influence of the guiding hand of him who, during the entire conflict, has been the Commander-in-Chief of all the forces, effecting these great victories, whether in the field, upon the sea, or in the council chamber.

While the precedents established by the diplomatic customs of the United States have been followed, more concise verbiage has been used, and the methods of procedure prescribed, are far less complex than those provided for in any previous treaty by which territory has been acquired, or claims by the United States against foreign powers have been settled.

The admission by the treaty that the United States is to be bound by the obligations imposed by International Law in regard to the occupancy of Cuba, is a signal victory for the principles of the decision of disputes between nations by recognized rules of law; it is practically an admission that the right to settle matters by the final arbitrament of war, can only be resorted to after the failure of an attempt at settlement by peaceful means, and under the rules of International Law.

The treaty is as notably a triumph of diplomacy in regard to the provisions that are "conspicuous by their absence" as it is in regard to those which do appear.

The omission of any reference to any indebtedness of the former sovereign of the ceded territory was the result of a long diplomatic struggle, in which our Commissioners were completely victorious; and, taking into consideration that the title had been acquired by conquest prior to the cession made by the treaty, as is evidenced by the incorporation of the Protocol of August 12th in the treaty as a part thereof, and the continuance in force of its provisions, will effectually defeat any claim by foreign creditors that the United States have directly or indirectly assumed any financial obligation for existing in connecton with any of the ceded territory.

The renunciation by Spain of her sovereignty over the Island of Cuba, without naming any power in whose favor such renunciation is made, is accompanied by the admission that the United States are now in military occupancy thereof, and thereby the anarchical condition which might otherwise have ensued is entirely averted, and all possible trouble therefrom prevented.

The treaty briefly, but most effectually, provides for the future civil and political status of the inhabitants, by vesting in Congress, the right to define the civil and political status of all the natives, thus, in a single sentence of less than twenty words, completely wiping out all the doleful forbodings which have been made by the foes of expansion, on account of the danger involved in making several millions of native, and possibly uncivilized, inhabitants of the Philippines citizens of the United States.

This point has been so completely covered by the Commissioners, in so few words, that the position of the calamity criers must be rather mortifying, when they see the entire panorama of future mishaps, woes and miseries, which they had so confidently and eloquently conjured up, melt away into such thin mist that the mere fact of its existence will have been entirely forgotten, before there will even be time to ratify the treaty.

While considering the greater matters involved in the transfer of territory, the Commissioners have not neglected the lesser details of preservation of evidence and muniments of title, and of property, thus averting many of the difficulties which were encountered in the establishment of titles in territory previously acquired.

The granting of equal rights to Spanish ships in the ports of the ceded territory during the brief term of ten years, shows a proper regard for the continuance of mercantile connections, the sudden shattering of which might cause those financial embarrassments which often follow the breaking off of long-continued associations.

In fine, the treaty will be welcomed by all true-hearted citizens as the just, proper and honorable termination of the hostilities which were forced upon us, and which we would have avoided had we been able, but which all the higher motives and principles that should actuate any nation compelled us enter upon.

The long discussion in regard to the policy of "expansion" has ended. That is, it has ended so far as any practical bearing upon the result is concerned. Doubtless there will be many arguments advanced conclusively proving that expansion is not only inadvisable, but that it is also unconstitutional, but meanwhile the country *has expanded*, and the real question now before the nation, is not whether we shall take the ceded territories under our jurisdiction, but, now that we have taken them, how we shall best govern them, not only for the sake of ourselves, but of the additional one per cent of the inhabitants of the globe for whom we have rendered greater service in the past six months, than all other civilized nations have rendered during the past three centuries.

The question of the advisability of the war itself was discussed in the same spirit last spring. Thousands hoped and prayed that it would be averted even at the cost—not to use any harsher terms—of national apathy, but the moment that the crisis came and war became not only inevitable, but a fact—a condition, so to speak, and not a theory—the question of its advisability, and its propriety, was forgotten, and all were for the Country, all prayed for victory. Should it not be so even now? Should not every one urge the promptest ratification of this peace bringing treaty and so help the nation, and those who are charged with the direction of its government, not only to accept these added possessions, but also to sustain the added responsibilities, and so to show to the world at large—for it is watching us now even as it did when the

Constitution was first adopted—that we have expanded not only territorially, but also in dignity and honor, and that our Government is no more an experiment to-day in the wider sphere over which it nows extends, than it was when we first assumed the reins of self-control.

In one of those short and characteristic speeches, delivered by the President in his recent visit to the South, he asked: "Who will pull down the flag now that it has been raised?" and told the story of the color bearer, who had advanced in the thick of battle beyond the foremost fighting line, and on being ordered to bring the flag back to the line, replied: "I can't; bring the line up to the flag." The flag has been advancing beyond the old line, but the line has been brought up to it. But does not the flag also float above the line, as well as beyond it? A very short time ago, it seemed too far beyond us, but we caught up to it, and although the higher it waves above us, the harder it may be to reach it, still, as "he higher shoots, who aims a star, than ho who aims a tree," surely the results attained will be all the greater if the struggle is the harder. We have overcome difficulties before, but only when we met them, not when we avoided them—when we changed our policy, not when we continued it. Spain has never changed her policy.

To-day the pirates of the Barbary Powers would still be levying tribute on our merchant marine, as they did when Washington himself transmitted to the Senate one of those mortifying treaties for confirmation, with a statement of the price involved for obtaining it, had we not changed our policy and asserted our ability to bring the line up to the flag under the leadership of Decatur, Allen and other prototypes of Farragut and Dewey. To-day the ships of foreign powers would be searching our merchantmen and impressing our seamen as they did for years, had we not changed our policy of submission and asserted our rights upon the sea under the leadership of Madison in the Executive Mansion, of Clay in the Senate, who sounded the watchword, "Freedom of Trade and Our Sailors Rights," of Lawrence and Perry on the sea, and of Jackson on the land.

To-day slavery would be an institution flourishing not only in those States to which it was once confined, but spreading over all the territories to which it was extended by the decision in the Dred Scott Case, had we not changed our policy, and had not Lincoln, even after he stated in his inaugural address, that he had no purpose directly or indirectly to interfere with the institution of slavery in the States where it existed, and that he believed he had no lawful right, and had no inclination to do so, himself signed the Proclamation of Emancipation. But will any one dare to blame him for that inconsistency. Thank God! the courage of inconsistency triumphed over the cowardice of consistency; where would this country be now had Lincoln hesitated, if some one had shown him a list of George Washington's slaves? Will the bitterest foe of Expansion espouse the cause either of contraction, or of disintegration?

The "Destiny of the United States" is not a mere phrase—or a mere fancy it can not be dismissed with a sneer. John Adams saw it when, in 1787, he contemplated the union of the whole of North America—a sphere of power and influence which for that day, or even for this, is far beyond any that we have assumed, or even thought of, as yet. William H. Seward saw it when he made his great address at Sitka after the purchase of Alaska. Is our vision any dimmer than their's?

Surely our great advance has not been all by chance—surely thus far the Lord hath led us on, and surely He will not forsake us now.

Many dangers have been encountered, all have been overcome; the skies have at times been dark, but the clouds have rolled away; responsibilities have been added, but increased strength has been given to bear them; have we not the right, should we not have the faith, to judge the future by the past? At this joyful Christmas season, when gifts are being exchanged between all who love each other, let the gifts of loyalty and allegiance that we are receiving from the far off regions of the south, and of the east, and of the west, be reciprocated by gifts, from us to them, of cordial and affectionate welcome, and let us freely assume our

new responsibilities as we have assumed those that came to us in
the past, remembering that nothing brings its own reward so
surely and so completely as the prompt recognition, and faithful
performance of duty.

> In the beauty of the lilies Christ was born across the sea,
> With a glory in His bosom that transfigures you and me;
> As He died to make them holy, let us die to make men free,
> While God is marching on.

We have heard that before; we have sung the words, as
we have marched with the tune to victory. There is power still
in the words; there is music still in the notes; the flag is still before us, and the flag is still above us. Are we still marching
on?

In the brief time at the annotator's disposal—less than three
days having elapsed since the publication of the text of treaty—it
has been impossible to thoroughly collate all the legal and historical precedents which should be cited in order to make this a
complete work; but the publishers have thought the presentation,
in a concise form, of the treaty, annotated by references to the
legal precedents and the corresponding clauses in former treaties
relating to similar subjects, with a few facts of interest, in connection with the negotiation of the treaty and the decisions of the
Supreme Court in regard to the rights of this Government under
the Constitution, as well as under the rules of International Law,
would be of interest to the public, who are probably more thoroughly and intelligently interested on this occasion than they
have ever been before, and therefore this annotation is presented
without further apologies as to its defects and deficiencies.

CHARLES HENRY BUTLER.

1531 I Street, Washington, D. C.
December 23, 1898.

ARTICLE I.

Spain renounces all right of sovereignty over Cuba; whereas, said isle, when evacuated by Spain, is to be occupied by the United States; the United States, while the occupation continues, shall take upon themselves and fulfill the obligations which, by the fact of occupation, international law imposes on them for the protection of life and property.

Cuba was discovered by Columbus during his first voyage in 1492. In 1511, Diego Velasquez, on behalf of Don Diego Columbus, took formal possession of the Island; it is said that the ceremony included the cremating alive of a native chief at the stake, and that the victim on being urged to abjure his own gods and accept Christianity so that his soul might go to "regions of eternal bliss," asked if there were any Spaniards in those happy abodes, and on receiving an affirmative reply declined to accept the proffered reward for his abjuration, on the ground that he preferred to go somewhere else and avoid their society.

Cuba has an area of about 43,000 square miles, and is about the size of the State of Pennsylvania. There are about 30,000,-000 acres, of which less than 3,000,000 are now under cultivation.

The population at one time was estimated at nearly 2,000,000. About eighteen months ago it was estimated at 1,500,000. At the time of the declaration of war it was supposed to be less than 1,000,000; it is impossible to obtain any accurate estimates in this respect.

In 1538, Havana was burned by a French privateer, and the occurrence was repeated in 1554, immediately after which Morro Castle was built. In 1762, Lord Albemarle, with a fleet of two hundred sail and a land force of over 14,000, attacked Havana, and after a seige of two months captured the city, which, together with all the surrounding country, remained in the possession of

England for about a year thereafter, when the Treaty of Paris, February 10, 1763, restored the territory to Spain, who ceded Florida to England; France ceded Louisiana to Spain by the same treaty. Florida was subsequently re-ceded to Spain by England. From 1763, Cuba has remained under Spanish rule, until by the present Treaty of Paris her sovereignty in the Island has been terminated forever. (For brief histories of Cuba see The Island of Cuba, by Rowan and Ramsey, N. Y.; Henry Holt, 1897; The Story of Cuba, Her Struggles for Liberty, Murat Halstead, Chicago, 1897.)

Renunciation.— The treaty is silent as to the power in whose favor Spain renounces her sovereignty over Cuba. This was a wise move on the part of the United States Commissioners. The sovereignty over every portion of territory of the world is vested in the people living within natural geographical boundaries, except so far as it has become vested in some sovereign power, and when that power renounces such sovereignty it vests again in the inhabitants thereof; Spain by this renunciation having abandoned her sovereignty, it again returns to the inhabitants of Cuba; as there is no organized government there to succeed to that of Spain, the sovereignty vests in the people in the same manner as her relinquished sovereignty over the Spanish colonies in South America vested in the people of each colony respectively, who thereafter organized their own independent governments.

In the present instance, if it were not for the occupancy of the United States, this might result in anarchy; it is, however, a safe provision, in view of the fact that the United States are in complete control, and, under the rules of military occupancy, have the right, and are under the duty, of maintaining order.

At the proper time, and subject to such rules and provisions as the occupant shall, as it has a right to do, prescribe, the people of Cuba can determine what form of government will be assumed, and it will also properly be within the power of the military occupant to determine whether the people shall be permitted to govern themselves accordingly or not.

The advantage of the complete renunciation of Spanish sovereignty, without the same being made in favor of any particular government, will become very apparent when any attempt shall be made by holders of Spanish obligations of any nature, to charge them upon the territory of Cuba, or against any power governing the same.

No obligation of any kind can be created against a government which is entirely new, and which could not possibly be charged with any indebtedness, on account of its non-existence when the indebtedness was incurred, and without any formal assumption thereof on its part.

The Evacuation of Cuba by Spanish forces was provided for in the Protocol of August 12 (See *Appendix*); under which a special Commission, consisting of Major-Generals Wade, and Butler, and Admiral Sampson, with Mr. Charles W. Gould of New York City as counsel, has been in Cuba since September, 1898, attending to the evacuation by the Spanish forces.

As rapidly as the Spanish forces leave the Island and territory is evacuated, the United States forces take possession and the military rule extends over the additional territory.

The obligations which are imposed under International Law by the fact of occupation, and which are assumed by the United States, grow out of the right of conquest of territory by sovereign nations as the result of war; the rules of occupancy have been well established both by International Law and the rules specially adopted by the United States.

On the capture of Santiago, the President issued a proclamation relating to the government of the territory conquered and occupied (See Appendix hereto), and by a subsequent proclamations, the same rules have been extended to all the other occupied territory, as the same is evacuated by the Spanish troops, or the lines of the United States forces are extended.

Apart from these particular rules, General Order No. 100, A. G. O., 1863, prepared during the Civil War by General Francis Lieber, and revised by a Board of Officers of the United States

Army, provides generally for rules in regard to occupancy of conquered territory by the military forces of the United States.

The general rules of occupancy under International Law are well expressed by Major George B. Davis, formerly Judge Advocate U. S. A., in his "Outlines of International Law," (N. Y., 1887. See Secs. 37-38); in the same volume will be found as appendices General Order No. 100, as well as the proposed rules for the law of war on land (largely devoted to rules as to occupied territory) which were recommended for adoption by the Institute of International Law at the session in Oxford, September, 1880, and which were largely based on our own regulations.

Snow's "Cases on International Law" (Boston, 1893, pp. 364-385) contains reference to a number of cases on the subject of occupation, and the rights and duties of the occupant, and of the inhabitants; the same volume also contains as an appendix at page 532, the Instructions for United States Armies, and the proposed Code of the Institute of International Law; also references to the subject of Military Occupation and the general character of the right and jurisdiction of the conquerer in the following works of International Law: Hall (English), 462-497, in which the whole subject is treated in its various aspects; Halleck (English Edition), Vol. 2, pp. 444-479; Bluntschli, Articles 539-541; Calvo, Sec. 2166-2198; Woolsey, 252; Creasy, 502-516; Walker, 344-346; Phillimore, Vol. 3, 832-840.

Captain Edwin F. Glenn, Judge Advocate U. S. A., in his "Hand-Book of International Law" (St. Paul, Minn., 1895), devotes Chap. XV, pp. 216-225, to the subject of occupancy. He summarizes some of the rules as follows:

"When a hostile army possesses a territory of the enemy, to the extent that it exercises actual authority over it, either through force or the acquiescence of the inhabitants, this territory is said to be occupied. The extent of occupied territory is determined by the limits over which this authority is established and can be exercised. * * * The occupant has the right to exercise such control over the occupied territory and its inhabitants as may be required for his safety and the success of his operations. * * * Constructive occupation implies a liberal interpretation of the term territory, and that occupation is complete within the district forming an administrative unit, so soon as military resistance on the part of the organized forces of the state ceases, and notice is posted or given in some other manner at a given place. * * * All laws implying or importing obedience to the original sovereign are suspended. Certain acts not ordinarily punishable are rendered so. Summary punishment is authorized for certain acts, and the death penalty is awarded in certain cases, where the offense is such as to authorize such punishment by the laws and usages of war. * * * Occupation authorizes taking and exercising complete control of the administration, but the practice is to permit such native officials as may be deemed desirable to perform their duties under supervision of the military authorities, or officers appointed by the occupant. * * * The civil officers thus retained can be required to take an oath of obedience of fidelity to the new ruler during the occupation, and for refusing to do so may be expelled. * * * The invader should at as early a date as practicable inform the inhabitants of the extent of the occupied district and the extent of the forces he exercises, should take measures to secure public order and tranquility, should nullify or alter existing laws as little as practicable, should not commit wanton damage, and should protect public buildings, works of art, etc."

In August, 1870, the Crown Prince of Prussia, upon entering France, included the following in his proclamation:

"Military jurisdiction is established by this decree. It will be applicable to the entire extent of territory occupied by German troops, to every action tending to endanger the security of those troops, to causing them injury or lending assistance to the enemy. Military jurisdiction will be considered as in force and proclaimed through all the extent of the canton as soon as it is posted in any locality forming a part of it."

Area of Territory Occupied.—In the triangular contention for the ownership and control of Cuba during the past year, three governmental parties have been interested: Spain, which, acording to every rule of International Law, was the only

sovereign nation exercising any control thereover, until
the Declaration of War, the United States, which have
acted under the rules of International Law, as inter-
venors, and the so-called Cuban Republic, which has been con-
ducting an insurrection, but which has never been recognized or
accorded belligerent rights by either the United States or the
Spanish Government, or in fact by any government which, at the
present time, could clothe that organization with the character of
a government, possessing any sovereignty, or right of control over
any part of the Island of Cuba.

The United States, having exercised the lawful right of inter-
vention, acquired a military occupancy, as against the only
recognized sovereign power, first under the Protocol of August
12th (See Appendix) temporarily, and now, assuming its ratification, permanently under the Treaty of Paris. This occupancy,
under all of the rules of International Law, as expressed by all the leading writers, including those above cited, also
gives them such exclusive military jurisdiction over all the
inhabitants, that any uprising on their part, whether under the
leadership of the so-called Cuban Republic, or any organization
claiming governmental powers, would be an insurrection as
against the United States, and would entitle them to use, under
the direction of the President, as Commander-in-Chief, all
military and naval power which could be exercised in time of
war; any such uprising should not under the rules of International Law be recognized by other foreign powers, as war, any
more than the United States had the right to recognize belliger-
ency on the part of the Cuban insurgents.

These same remarks will apply, so far as any uprising is concerned, to the Fillipinos in the Philippine Islands, so long as that
territory continues under military government, i. e., until Congress shall legislate in regard thereto. After that, any uprising
would be exactly the same as an uprising in Alaska or any other
territory of the United States.

As the sovereignty of Spain extended over the entire Island of
Cuba and all of the islands adjacent thereto, so the occupancy of

the United States, having been recognized by the former sovereign, extends co-terminously with the extent of Spain's former sovereignty to the fullest extent, and the entire Island of Cuba, the Isle of Pines, and all of the various "Gardens of the King," and Archipelagos lying adjacent, to what might be called in this respect, the mainland, are equally brought under the jurisdiction of the military power of the United States, to be exercised by, or through, the President as Commander-in-Chief.

Title to Cuba Not Acquired.—Under the rules of International Law no permanent title is acquired by military occupation.

While this is generally true, there is still a prescriptive title which, after a long period of non-resistance to military occupancy might ripen into actual sovereignty, but it is always subject to an act of reclamation by the original sovereign, and, therefore, it is as difficult a title to sustain under International Law, until ratified by a treaty, as is a title by adverse possession between individuals, until assured by a quit claim from the original owner.

Constitutional questions in this respect have arisen heretofore in regard to territory occupied by the United States.

The Supreme Court has decided that actual ownership of territory and extension of the boundaries of the United States can not be effected by the President alone in his military capacity as Commander-in-Chief, but only by legislative action; but it has, also held that territory occupied by conquest is, as to all the world, part of the United States, although it exists under a peculiar status as to the United States themselves, and remains to a certain extent foreign territory.

In *Fleming* vs. *Page* (9 Howard, U. S. Reports, p. 603), Chief Justice Taney, in defining the relations of Tampico, a Mexican port captured by United States troops, and occupied during the war, but afterwards surrendered to Mexico by the treaty of peace, in 1848, says:

"By the laws and usages of nations conquest is a valid title, while the victor maintains the exclusive possession of the conquered country. The citizens of no other nation, therefore, had a right to enter it without the permission of

American authorities, nor to hold intercourse with its inhabitants, nor to trade with them. As regarded all other nations, it was a part of the United States, and belonged to them as exclusively as the territory included in our established boundaries. * * * While the territory was occupied by our troops they were in an enemy's country, and not in their own; the inhabitants were still foreigners and enemies, and owed to the United States nothing more than the submission and obedience—sometimes called temporary allegiance—which is due from a conquered enemy, when he surrenders to a force which he is unable to resist. But the boundaries of the United States, as they existed when war was declared, were not extended by the conquest; nor could they be regulated by the varying incidents of war and be enlarged or diminished as the armies of either side advanced or retreated. They remained unchanged.

The President, as Commander-in-Chief of the Army, has full power over the occupied territory, and this power continues as long as the military occupancy continues, irrespective of whether any treaty is signed or not.

"The President shall be Commander-in-Chief of the Army and Navy of the United States and of the militia of the several States when called into actual service of the United States." (Constitution of the U. S., Art. 2, Sec. 2.) The decisions of the Supreme Court relating to this subject have been collated in Black's "Hand Book of Constitutional Law." (St. Paul, Minn., 1895), see pp. 95-97 and cases cited, as follows: *U. S. vs. Eliasson*, 16 Peters, 291; *U. S. vs. Freeman*, 3 Howard, 556; *The Prize Cases*, 2 Black, 635; *Fleming vs. Page*, 9 Howard, 603; *Totten vs. U. S.*, 105; *The Grape Shot*, 9 Wall, 192; *Allen vs. Colby*, 47 N. H., 514; on page 97 he says:

"In virtue of his rank as the head of the forces, he has certain powers and duties with which Congress can not interfere. For instances, he may regulate the movements of the Army and the stationing of them at various posts. So also he may direct the movements of the vessels of the navy, sending them wherever in his judgment it is expedient. Neither here, nor in a state of war, is there any necessary conflict. The President has no power to declare war. That belongs exclusively to Congress. But when war has been declared, or when it is recognized as actually existing, then his functions as Commander-in-Chief become of the highest importance, and his operations in that character are entirely beyond the control of the legislature. It is true that Congress shall alone raise and support the army and provide and maintain the navy, and it is true that the power of furnishing or withholding the necessary means and supplies may give it an indirect influence on the conduct of the war. But the supreme command belongs to the President alone. In theory, he plans all campaigns, establishes the blockades and sieges, directs all marches, fights all battles."

It will be remembered that the plenary power with which the President is clothed as Commander-in-Chief proceeds from a clause in the Constitution, which was framed by a convention over which George Washington himself presided, and he well knew how necessary it was that the Commander-in-Chief of the Army should not be hampered by any restrictions whatsoever.

Until Congress acts, the mere execution and ratification of peace does not in any way interrupt the military government. That continues until Congress assumes jurisdiction and control by extending the laws of the United States over conquered or occupied territory.

This point was settled by the Supreme Court in the case of *Cross vs. Harrison* 16 Howard, 164), and on this question the Court says:

"The formation of the civil government in California, when it was done, was the lawful exercise of a belligerent right over a conquered territory. It was the existing government when the territory was ceded to the United States, as a conquest, and did not cease as a matter of course, or as a consequence of the restoration of peace; it was rightfully continued after peace was made with Mexico until Congress legislated otherwise, under its Constitutional power to dispose of and make all needful rules and regulations respecting the territory or other property belonging to the United States.

"The tonnage duties and duties upon foreign goods imported into San Francisco were legally demanded and lawfully collected by the civil governor, whilst war continued, and afterwards, from the ratification of the treaty of peace until the revenue system of the United States was put into practical operation in California under the acts of Congress passed for that purposes."

Obligations Imposed by International Law.—International law not only confers the right of military government, but also imposes the obligation of maintaining order upon the occupant of territory conquered or ceded as a result of war.

In this respect Hall says (Sec. 160):

"Though the fact of occupation imposes no duties upon the inhabitants of the occupied territory, the invader himself is not left equally free. As it is a consequence of his own acts that the regular government of the country is suspended, he is bound to take whatever means are required for the security of public order; and as his presence, so long as it is based upon occupation, is confessedly temporary, and his rights of control spring only from the necessity of the case, he is also bound, over and above the limitations before stated, to alter or override the existing laws as little as possible, whether he is acting in his own or the general interest. As moreover his rights belong to him only that he may bring the war to a successful issue, it is his duty not to do acts which injure individuals, without facilitating his operations, or putting a stress upon his antagonists. Thus, though he may make use of or destroy both public and private property for any object connected with the war, he must not commit wanton damage, and he is even bound to protect public buildings, works of art, libraries and museums."

In regard to this, see also Art. 39 of General Order No. 100, 1863; Project of the Declaration of Brussels, Art. 5; Manual of the Institute of International Law, Art. 42-49; Bluntschli, Sec. 647.

Beyond these obligations to maintain law and order, as any civilized government ought to do, there does not seem to be any obligation imposed by International Law upon the occupant of territory.

With the obligations thus imposed, the correlative grant of power is implied, and under all the rules, the invader and occupant has the right to impose contributions and requisitions if necessary, or to raise funds by the preferable course, which has been pursued in the present instance (see Appendix), of levying duties upon imports and exports, the proceeds of which belong to the invader for the purpose of maintaining his army, and law and order thereby. This rule has been settled by the Supreme Court in the cases of *Fleming* vs. *Page*, 9 Howard, 603, and *Cross* vs. *Harrison*, 16 Howard, 164, above referred to.

ARTICLE II.

Spain cedes to the United States the Island of Porto Rico and the other islands now under her sovereignty in the West Indies, and the isle of Guam, in the archipelago of the Marianas or Ladrones.

Porto Rico, or as it is also spelt, Puerto Rico, is an island in the West Indies, which ranks in size as the fourth of the Greater Antilles, but which takes the first place for density of population and general prosperity, as stated by Reclus in his Universal Geography (English Edition, Volume 17, page 423). The population in 1765 was somewhat less than 45,000. In 1891, it exceeded 820,000.

It is 108 miles long, 37 broad, has an area of 3,530 square miles (about three times the size of Long Island). The island was discovered by Columbus in 1493, and was conquered by the Spaniards under Ponce de Leon 1509-18. During this period nearly the whole native population was exterminated. It has since been held by Spain. Slavery was abolished in 1873. (Johnson's Encyclopedia.)

The Isle of Guam, in the archipelago of the Marianas or Ladrones, is the largest island in a group of 17 islands, which stretches north and south in the Pacific Ocean for a total distance of 600 miles. The land area of the entire group is somewhat over 500 square miles. There is an annual postal service with Manila. Population in 1875 was estimated at 9,000 for the entire archipelago, of which about 7,500 were supposed to be in Guam.

These islands were the first Pacific Ocean group which Magellan met in 1521 on his voyage around the world. Ten days after he sighted them he reached the Philippines and died.

They were first called Ladrones, which, being translated, means "robbers." They were subsequently named in 1564 Mariana, after the Austrian wife of Philip II. They are about 1,200 miles this side of the Philippines. They have been held by Spain ever since their discovery by Magellan, and their subsequent occupation, in 1564, at the same time when the Philippines were occupied.

The evacuation of Porto Rico was provided for by the protocol of August 12th (see appendix); a special Commission consisting of Major-General John R. Brooke, Rear Admiral W. S. Schley and Brigadier-General W. W. Gordon, conducted the proceedings; the evacuation was completed by the departure of the Spanish army, and the transfer of possessions of the United States was evidenced by the raising of the stars and stripes October 18th, since which time the island has been under the complete military control of this Government.

Right of One Sovereign Power to Cede Territory to Another Sovereign Power. This right is discussed in Hall's International Law, Section 9, pages 47-50. He defines it as follows (p. 47):

> "The rights of a state with respect to property consist of the right to acquire territory, in being entitled to peaceable possession and enjoyment of that which it has duly obtained, and in the faculty of using its property as it chooses and alienating it at will. * * * The principle that the wishes of the population are to be consulted when the territory which they inhabit is ceded, has not yet been adopted into International Law, and can not be adopted into it until title by conquest has disappeared."

He cites the cessions of Savoy to France, the Ionian Islands to Greece, Venetia to Italy, and other European cessions, and further says (p. 49):

> "States being the sole international units, the inhabitants of a ceded territory, whether acting as an organized body or

as an unorganized mass of individuals, have no more power to confirm or reject the action of their state than is possessed by a single individual. An act, on the other hand, done by the state as a whole is, by the very conception of a state, binding upon all the members of it."

The following is a citation from an eminent authority:

"I need not dwell upon the right to transfer territory, or in other words, to put an end to all dominion over them, for acquisition on the part of one nation implies transfer, or end of dominion, by another."— John Norton Pomeroy's Lectures on International Law. Edited by Theo. S. Woolsey, Boston, 1886, p. 198.

In Halleck's International Law, San Francisco Edition, 1861, at page 125, the rule is stated:

"A state being regarded in our law as a body politic or distinct moral being, naturally sovereign and independent, it is considered capable of the same rights, duties and obligations with respect to other states as individuals with respect to other individuals. Among the most important of these natural rights, is that of acquiring, possessing, and enjoying property. * * * A sovereign has the same absolute right to dispose of its territorial, or rather public, property, as it has to acquire such property."

Halleck thinks that in some cases the consent of the governed is necessary before the transfer of allegiance can take place, but he shows, however, that there are numerous examples of treaties of sale, and cites a number of them on pages 128 and 129, and states that in some instance territories have even been mortgaged, and bought in thereafter, and that furthermore, it has been the custom "to dispose of sovereignties and dominions by deeds of gift and by bequests."

The Right of the United States to Acquire Territory has been the subject of a vast amount of debate in Congress and in the papers. There are some who deny the right, but it is difficult to conceive on what authority. The Supreme Court has decided that the *United States is a nation*, and as such has all the rights of sovereignty that every other sovereign nation has, and can exercise them just as broadly, including the right of acquisition of territory.

Senator O. H. Platt, of Connecticut, delivered an able address on this subject in the Senate, December 19th, 1898, and referred to most of the authorities. (Cong. Record, p.321, et seq.) In this respect he quoted from Judge Gray's opinion in one of the *Chinese Exclusion Cases*, 149 U. S., 711, as follows:

"The United States are a sovereign and independent nation, and are vested by the Constitution with the entire control of international relations and with all the powers of government necessary to maintain that control and to make it effective. The only government of this country, which other nations recognize or treat with, is the Government of the Union, and the only American flag that is known throughout the world is the flag of the United States."

The Senator then continued:

"The doctrine was denied by Hayne. It was triumphantly asserted by Webster in his great debate, in which he first made it plain to the American people that the United States lacked no element of nationality. It was denied in the nullification acts. It was triumphantly asserted by Jackson, when he threatened to hang the originator of the acts, and so cowed the incipient rebellion. It was denied in the ordinances of secession; but it was again gloriously asserted by Abraham Lincoln, when he issued his call for 75,000 volunteer troops to preserve the Union, and the people gloriously responded. It has been written in the books. It has been written in the published utterances of statesmen from the time when the people of the States made our Constitution down to the present time.

"But, Mr. President, it has been otherwise written. It has been written in the blood which deluged the battlefields of the Civil War for four long years. It has been written with the sword upon the heart of every true American citizen. It has been written on the mourning weeds of the widows who lost husbands, of the mothers who lost children, of the children who lost fathers. It is too late to deny it, Mr. President; it is time to believe in it with a living, saving faith, from which all doubt is eradicated."

As to right of acquisition and the right to govern territory when acquired, see also: Pomeroy's Constitution, 494-498, *Jones vs. U. S., (the Narassa Islands case)* 137, U. S., pp. 202-212;

Justice Miller's Lectures on the Constitution, 35, 36, 55, 57; Justice Curtis' Opinion (*Dred Scott case*), 19 Howard, 612-614.

These cases and opinions are all based upon the broad declaration made by the Chief Justice Marshall, in 1824, in *American Ins. Co.* vs. *Canter*: 1 Peters, 511, p. 542: "The Constitution confers absolutely on the Government of the Union the power to make war and to make treaties; consequently that government possesses the power of acquiring territory either by conquest or by treaty."

Cessions of Territory Made to the United States.--This is the second cession of territory made by Spain to the United States, and, at least the eleventh acquisition of territory, by the United States, increasing its original area of less than a million square miles to its present magnificent domain three times as large in area and over fifteen times as great in population: the first cession made by Spain was in 1819 under the Adams-de Onis Treaty, by which Spain ceded Florida to the United States, in consideration of $5,000,000, which was the liquidated amount of the claims owed by Spain to citizens of the United States for depredations upon our commerce and in territory adjoining Florida.

The United States has Acquired Territory as Follows: By the Treaty of Peace with Great Britain after the Revolutionary War, when the original boundaries of the United States were fixed, and Great Britain renounced all jurisdiction over the territory therein, which included not only the thirteen original States themselves, but also what was afterwards known as the Northwest Territory; the original territory extended from what is now Canada on the north—the boundary line between which and the United States has been fixed by several subsequent treaties and arbitrations—to the northerly line of Florida on the south; from the Atlantic on the east, to the Mississippi on the west, containing about eight hundred and twenty-five thousand square miles. (U. S. Treaty, Vol., p. 375.)

The acquisition of territory since that time have been:

(1.) *Louisiana*, consisting, including Oregon, the discovery and occupation of which grew out of this acquisition, of over a million square miles, ceded by France to the United States under treaty of April 30, 1803, ratified October 21, 1803, by which France, under Napoleon Bonaparte as First Consul, through Barbé Marbois, ceded the territory for 60,000,000 francs, and the relinquishment of claims amounting to 20,000,000 francs. (U. S. Treaty, Volume 331-342). Well did Mr. Livingston exclaim to Mr. Monroe, as they arose from signing the treaty: "We have lived long, but this is the noblest work of our lives."

(2.) *Florida*, consisting of about sixty thousand square miles, under the treaty with Spain in 1819, above referred to (U. S. Treaty, Volume, p. 1016).

(3.) *Oregon* and adjoining territory was acquired by the United States under the general rules of discovery and occupancy, based upon the discovery of the mouth of the Columbia River by Captain Gray, master of the good ship Columbia, entering from the Pacific in 1797; by Lewis and Clark as explorers in an expedition fitted by the United States proceeding from the east about 1804; and by the erection of the furring post by John Jacob Astor at Astoria in 1811. The title to Oregon was subsequently confirmed by treaty with Spain in 1819, so far as the northerly line of the Spanish possessions was concerned, not however in the nature of cession, but only of quit claim. (U. S. Treaty, Volume, p. 1016.) The area of territory north of California and east of the Rockies is about three hundred and fifty thousand square miles.

(4.) *Texas*, with an area of over a quarter of a million square miles, in 1845, by joint resolution, adopted by both Houses of Congress, after a proposed treaty had failed, was admitted as a State, the legislature of the Republic of Texas having accepted the terms and conditions contained in a joint resolution adopted by Congress. (For resolution and proclamation see U. S. Statutes at Large for 1845.)

(5.) *California, Colorado, Nevada, Utah, New Mexico*, and parts of Arizona and other States, over five hundred thousand square miles in all, were acquired under the Treaty of Guadaloupe-

Hidalgo with Mexico in 1848, at the termination of the Mexican War, and in consideration of $15,000,000 paid to Mexico under somewhat similar circumstances as the $20,000,000 is to be paid to Spain under the present treaty. (U. S. Treaty, Volume, p. 687.)

(6.) *Horse Shoe Reef in Lake Erie*, was ceded to the United States by Great Britain in 1850, without any actual consideration, but under agreement that the United States would erect and maintain a light-house thereon. (U. S. Treaty, Volume, p. 444.)

(7.) *The Narassa Islands*, near Hayti, and the other *Guano Islands* in the Pacific Ocean, have been taken and occupied by the United States by discovery in pursuance of statutes of the United States made in regard thereto (U. S. Revised Statutes, Secs. 5770-5778); *The Midway Islands*, situated in the Pacific Ocean, about half way between Hawaii and Japan, were discovered by citizens, and afterwards formally occupied in 1867 by the naval forces of the United States under the direction of Secretary Gideon Welles. (See Senator Platt's Speech, Senate, December 19, 1898, Congress. Rec., p. 325.)

(8.) *Part of Arizona and New Mexico*, consisting of nearly fifty thousand square miles, were acquired under treaty negotiated by James Gadsden in 1853, and for which the sum of $10,000,000 was paid to Mexico. (U. S. Treaty Volume, p. 694.)

(9.) *Alaska*, in 1867, became United States territory by a treaty negotiated between William H. Seward, as Secretary of State, and Edward Stockel, Russian Ambassador to the United States, and which conveyed to this Government all of the Russian Possessions in America, consisting of over half a million square miles, and to which the name of Alaska has since been applied, for $7,200,000. (U. S. Treaty, Volume, p. 939.)

(10.) *Hawaii* was annexed by a joint resolution adopted by the Congress of the United States, and approved July 7, 1898, the terms of which were accepted by the legislative body of Hawaii shortly thereafter, and by which joint action, all of the islands forming the sovereignty of Hawaii, and which were formerly known as the Sandwich Islands, became a part of the terri tory, but not as a State, of the United States, and subject to the terms of the joint resolution. (Public Resolution, H. R. No. 51, July 7, 1898.)

(See the last map of the United States, published by the Government, for most of these additions of territory, showing their area and geographical locations.)

ARTICLE III.

Spain cedes to the United States the archipelago known as the Philippine Islands, which comprise the islands situated between the following lines: A line which runs west to east near the twentieth parallel of north latitude, across the centre of the navigable canal of Bachi, from the 118th to the 127th degrees of longitude east of Greenwich; from here to the width of the 127th degree of longitude east to parallel 4 degrees 45 seconds of north latitude; from here following the parallel of north latitude 4 degrees 45 seconds to its intersection with the meridian of longitude, 119 degrees 35 seconds east from Greenwich; from here following the meridian of 119 degrees 35 seconds east to the parallel of latitude 7 degrees 40 seconds north; from here following the parallel of 7 degrees 40 seconds north to its intersection with 116 degrees longitude east; from here along a straight line to the intersection of the 10th parallel of latitude north with the 118th meridian east, and from here following the 118th meridian to the point whence began this demarkation. The United States shall pay to Spain the sum of $20,000,-000 within three months after the interchange of the ratification of the present treaty.

The Philippine Islands.—Most of the following data is taken from a book entitled, "Military Notes on the Philippines," published in September, 1898, as Document No. 81, of the Military Information Division, by the Advocate General's Office, War Department.

The islands were discovered by Magellan in 1521; in 1564 the archipelago received its present name, in honor of King Philip II. The group is composed of about 2,000 islands, but many of them are very small, and the exact number is unknown. Spain did not acquire actual possession of the islands, although several expeditions were made, until 1564; in 1581 the city of Manila was founded. The Portuguese, Dutch and Chinese have, during the past three centuries, all made efforts to displace the Spaniards and occupy these islands, but they have all failed to do so. In 1762, the same year in which Havana was taken by Lord Albemarle, Manila was also taken by the English and held for a ransom of a million pounds sterling, which appears, however, to have been remitted, and the islands were subsequently returned to Spain.

The area covered by the archipelago is definitely described in the treaty, so far as latitude and longitude is concerned, but it is somewhat differently described in the Military Notes. The treaty description, however, will control, to the extent of Spain's sovereignty thereover.

According to the map in the Military Notes, the archipelago extends about 1,000 miles north and south, and 600 miles east and west.

The largest island is Luzon, upon which the city of Manila is located, and which has an area of 41,000 square miles (about 2,000 square miles less than Cuba, and about equal in area to the State of Virginia.)

Mindanao, next in size, covers about 37,500 square miles. The five next in size have an area of over 10,000 square miles each. The total estimated area is somewhat over 114,000 square miles, about equal to the area of Arizona.

On page 20 it is stated that the Spanish statistics are notoriously unreliable, and no accurate census has ever been taken, but that the population is estimated at about 8,000,000, of which the bulk is of Malay origin. Probably there are not more than 15,000 or 20,000 people of pure Spanish blood on the island, the majority of these being at Manila.

It has also been stated that there are over 1,000,000 natives, who have Chinese blood in them, and over 100,000 Chinese in Manila, which has a total population of 400,000; probably one-half of the entire population of the archipelago live on the Island of Luzon.

On page 25, it is stated that the total imports in 1896 were $10,631,250, and the exports were $20,175,000, and the public revenue was about $12,000,000 of which the larger part is raised from direct taxation, customs, monopolies and lotteries.

$20,000,000; as to the amount to be paid by the United States, see notes under Art. VII, post.

ARTICLE IV.

The United States shall, during the term of ten years, counting from the interchange of the ratifications of the treaty, admit to the ports of the Philippine Islands Spanish ships and merchandise under the same conditions as the ships and merchandise of the United States.

Privileges of Spanish Vessels in Ports of Ceded Territory. — This is not an unusual clause in cession treaties. The business interests of the inhabitants, who have, of course, had connections extending over long periods with people in their home country, demand that those connections should not be too speedily terminated, and certainly such a clause not only benefits the citizens of the ceding Government, but also inures to the benefit of the new owner, by preventing those mercantile collapses, which are so apt to follow interruption of long-established commercial associations.

By the Louisiana treaty with France (U. S. Treaty, Volume, page 333) special privileges were extended to the vessels of France and Spain, or any of their colonies, putting them upon an equal footing with vessels of the United States for the term of twelve years, commencing three months after the exchange of ratifications, the treaty also expressly providing that such privileges should not be given to any other nation.

In the treaty with Spain of 1819 (U. S. Treaty, Volume, p. 1021) the United States agreed "that Spanish vessels coming laden only with provisions of Spanish growth or manufacture directly from the ports of Spain, or of her colonies, shall be admitted for the term of twelve years to the ports of Pensacola and St. Augustine, without paying other or higher duties on their cargoes, or of tonnage, than will be paid by the vessels of the United States. During the same term no other nation shall enjoy the same privileges within the ceded territories. The twelve years shall commence three months after the exchange of the ratification of this treaty."

In the treaty with Russia of 1824 (U. S. Treaty, Volume, page 932) which fixed the southern boundary of what afterwards became Alaska, it was "understood that during a term of ten years, counting from the signature of the convention, the ships of both powers, or which belong to their citizens or subjects, respectively, may reciprocally frequent without any hindrance whatever, the interior seas, gulfs, harbors and creeks upon the coast mentioned in the preceding article, for the purpose of fishing and trading with the natives of the land."

ARTICLE V.

The United States, on the signing of the present treaty, shall transport to Spain at their cost the Spanish soldiers whom the American forces made prisoners of war when Manila was captured. The arms of these soldiers shall be returned to them. Spain, on the interchange of the ratification of the present treaty, shall proceed to evacuate the Philippine Islands, as also Guam, on conditions similar to those agreed to by the commissions named to concert the evacuation of Porto Rico and the other islands in the Western Antilles, according to the protocol of August 12, 1898, which shall continue in force until its terms have been completely complied with. The term within which the evacuation of the Philippine Islands and Guam shall be completed shall be fixed by both governments. Spain shall retain the flags and stands of colors of the warships not captured, small arms, cannons of all calibers, with their carriages and accessories, powders, munitions, cattle, material and effects of all kinds belonging to the armies of the sea and land of Spain in the Philippines and Guam. The pieces of heavy caliber which are not field artillery mounted in fortifications and on the coasts, shall remain in their places for a period of six months from the interchange of the ratifications of the present treaty, and the United States may, during that period, buy from Spain said material, if both governments arrive at a satisfactory agreement thereon.

Evacuation of the Philippines.—This article provides that the details of the evacuation of the Philippines shall be conducted on conditions similar to those already provided for the evacuation of Cuba, and Porto Rico, under the terms of the Protocol of August 12, 1898.

Any question that possibly the Protocol might be construed as a war measure, and the temporary or preliminary relations thereby created, terminated with the ratification of the treaty of peace, is obviated by continuing it in force until all of its terms shall have been finally complied with, even though the treaty shall meanwhile be ratified.

The Commission, under which Porto Rico was to be evacuated, has performed its duties and is now *functus officio*, but the Commission superintending the evacuation of Cuba is still engaged in performing the duties devolving upon its members, and they may not be completed until after the ratification of the treaty.

The other provisions of this article relate to the special privileges granted to Spain of retaining the uncaptured flags and colors, together with some of their military and naval supplies.

A very sensible provision, however, is made with regard to the heavy armament, as during the next six months it will doubtless be possible to agree upon the basis of compensation which will make it both advantageous to the United States to buy, and not worth while for Spain to incur the expense of removing, the heavy articles of ordnance still remaining on the Islands.

ARTICLE VI.

Spain, on signing the present treaty, shall place at liberty all prisoners of war and all those detained or imprisoned for political offenses in consequence of the insurrections in Cuba and the Philippines, and of the war with the United States. Reciprocally, the United States shall place at liberty all prisoners of war made by the American forces, and shall negotiate for the liberty of all Spanish prisoners in the power of the insurgents in Cuba and the Philippines. The Government of the United States shall transport at its cost to Spain, and the government of Spain shall transport at its cost to the United States, Cuba, Porto Rico and the Philippines, conformably to the situation of their respective dwellings, the prisoners placed or to be placed at liberty in virtue of this article.

Release of Prisoners.—In providing by this article for the mutual release of prisoners, Spain does not assume any responsibility, or undertake to perform any arduous duties, as the number of prisoners, which they have been able to take during the war, has been rather small, but there are prisoners confined in Cuba and the Philippines for political offenses, and those will all be released; even if this were not provided for in the treaty, the United States would be able to liberate those who have been confined for political offenses, or for that matter, for any reason whatever, as soon as the armies of occupation are in complete possession.

The United States assume no responsibility for any prisoners not in their own possession, who, of course, will be at once released, except so far as they are obliged to *negotiate* "for the liberty of all Spanish prisoners in the power of the insurgents in Cuba and the Philippines." As the United States will be the paramount power in Cuba, and the Philippines, they will be able, as soon as Spain has withdrawn, to assert whatever power is necessary over the insurgents to obtain the liberation of those prisoners, and if necessary they can resort to the most stringent methods in order to accomplish the purpose.

The Commissioners of the United States in this article have also shown the disposition of this Government to afford to a conquered enemy every facility for promptly obliterating all remembrances of the war, and of once more assuming a peaceful course of government, and in agreeing to transport the prisoners to their respective homes at its own expense they have simply provided for the repetition of the hitherto almost unparalleled act of generosity on the part of one belligerent toward another during actual hostilities, which occurred after the capture of Santiago.

Mutual Renunciation of Claims.—Sovereign nations have the right to renounce claims not only for themselves, but also on

account of their subjects, as against each other, and it is optional.
whether or not they will, themselves, liquidate the claims of their
own citizens.

This arises from the fact that a sovereign state can not be sued
without its own consent, and the only obligation which the United
States will have under this clause will be whatever Congress
shall see fit to assume on behalf of the Government towards citizens of the United States.

Citizens of the United States, however, can undoubtedly rely
upon the fairness and justness of Congress, and the amount
which eventually may have to be paid to liquidate any just
claims will practically be added to the price expressed in the
treaty for the ceded territory.

At the present time probably over three hundred claims have
been filed in the State Department for amounts aggregating in all
possibly over twenty millions, but, of course, all of the amounts
are "outside" figures, many of them being in the nature of claims
for unliquidated damages, such as detention in prison, death of
relatives, etc., and the actual aggregate amount of claims involved is probably a comparatively small percentage of their al-
leged "face values" as filed.

The extinguishment of claims of one nation against another is
a usual clause in treaties of this nature.

By Articles XIII, XIV and XV of the treaty of Guadaloupe-
Hidalgo, with Mexico, in 1848, the United States engaged to
assume and pay the claims of their citizens against the Mexican
Republic, including those under arbitration, pursuant to previous
treaties (U. S. Treaty, Volume 687-688), "and exonerating Mex-

> ico from all demands on account of the claims of citizens of
> the United States mentioned in the preceding article, and
> considering them entirely and forever cancelled, whatever
> their amount may be, undertook to make satisfaction for the
> same to an amount not exceeding three and a quarter mil-
> lions of dollars."

By Article XI of the Adams-de Onis treaty with Spain, in
1819, "The United States exonerating Spain from all demands

in future on account of the claims of their citizens to which
the renunciations herein contained extend, and considering
them entirely cancelled, undertake to make satisfaction for
the same to an amount not exceeding five millions of dollars."

In both of these instances it seems that the limitation of
amount was for the protection of the United States and not for
the foreign powers, as there was no provision for the foreign
powers being obliged to pay any additional amount (U. S.
Treaty, Volume, page 1020).

Under the treaty of Washington with Great Britain, of 1871,
the payments by the respective governments, one to the other, of
the awards of the tribunals established by the treaty were to act
as full perfect and final settlements of all the claims referred to in
the treaty, and the contracting powers further engaged that
"every such claim, whether the same may or may not have
been presented to the notice of, made, preferred or laid before the tribunal or board, shall from and after the conclusion of the proceedings of the tribunal or board be considered and treated as finally settled, barred and thenceforth
inadmissable."

The effect, therefore, of the first clause of this article is to entirely obliterate all claims which any citizen of the United States
may have against the Government of Spain of any kind or nature
whatsoever, provided it arose within the time mentioned in the
article, and a similar state of affairs exists in regard to the claim
of any citizen of Spain against the United States. This clause,
however, does not in any respect relate to claims of private citizens of one country against the other. That subject will be referred to in the notes under Article VIII and at the end of the
treaty.

ARTICLE VII.

*Spain and the United States mutually renounce by the present
treaty all claim to national or private indemnity of whatever kind
of one government against the other government which may have
arisen from the beginning of the last insurrection in Cuba, anterior
to the interchange of the ratifications of the present treaty, as also*

to all indemnity as regards costs occasioned by the war. The
United States shall judge and settle the claims of its citizens against
Spain which are renounced in this article.

Waiver of Indemnity by the United States.—This article,
however, does relate to all claims which the Government of the
United States might have against Spain. or *vice versa*, if any
could even be supposed to exist.

By this clause the United States waives the claim of any indemnity whatever against Spain, either in the nature of redress
for injury to private citizens, or for the expense of preparing for,
and maintaining the war, or for the loss of the Maine.

In this respect the United States has adhered to its own customs, instituted as far back as 1803, when, by the Louisiana
Treaty they paid for the territory on the condition that part
should be applied to the payment of claims existing in favor of
Americans against the French Government for spoliations prior
to 1800, and which was afterwards followed in the Adams-de
Onis treaty of 1819, with Spain. when Florida was accepted at a stipulated price of $5,000,000, and the claims of the
citizens effaced. and which was also pursued in 1848, when Cali
fornia. Nevada. New Mexico. and other territory were accepted
as indemnity for the Mexican war, and"the sum of $15,000,000
paid as representing an excess of value over the cost of the war.
but Mexico was obliged to pay $3,250,000 for claims of our citi-
zens against that power.

Other nations have not exercised the same leniency towards
their defeated enemies. In 1870 Germany exacted from France
not only Alsace and Lorraine, but 5,000,000,000 francs cash indemnity, and only accepted that amount after having impover-
ished the territory by the requisitions which had been levied
upon it for the support of the invading army. A single day's re-
quisition of the German Army when it occupied Versailles. is
stated by Halleck (Baker's edition, Vol. 2, p. 111; see also T. J.
Lawrence, p. 375) as being 120,000 loaves of bread, 80.000
pounds of meat, 90,000 pounds of oats. 27,000 pounds of rice.
7.000 pounds of coffee, 4,000 pounds of salt. 20,000 litres of

wine, and 500,000 cigars, all of which the inhabitants were forced to furnish in addition to the indemnity.

The largest indemnity most recently exacted was at the end of the Japan-Chinese war, when Japan not only retained the captured Island of Formosa, but received a cash indemnity of nearly two hundred million dollars, which probably would have been far greater had it not been for friendly offices of our Minister to China, Colonel Charles A. Denby, who, to some extent, acted as a mediator, and the able and successful efforts of ex-Secretary of State John W. Foster, who was not then connected with the United States Government, and who represented the Chinese Government in the peace negotiations, and materially reduced the indemnity from the amount originally demanded.

Under all the established rules of International Law, the United States would have been justified in exacting an indemnity equal to the entire expense of preparing for, and maintaining, the war, all the claims of their citizens, the estimated cost of occupation and the transformation of the country into revenue producing territory, together, if they saw fit, with an amount to be fixed by themselves in the way of punitive damages, to say nothing in regard to the "Maine."

Whatever, therefore, these items would amount to, together with the $20,000,000 stipulated to be paid by the treaty, can be considered as the total cost of the Philippine Islands, Porto Rico and Guam.

The final clause of Article VII places the question of adjudication, and settlement of the claims of its citizens against Spain entirely in the hands of the United States.

As above stated, that matter will be disposed by Congressional action. If that body follows the precedents already established in the cases of the French spoliation claims, claims against Spain for depredations in, and near, Florida, claims against Mexico, and the distribution of the Alabama award, a commission will be appointed which can take proof as to all the claims of United States citizens, or a special court may be established for the purpose, or the claimants may be permitted to establish their rights according to laws to be enacted before the regular Court of Claims. Proceedings will differ from some of those provided in regard to the other cessions and settlements of claims, however, in that the Commissioners and Judges will undoubtedly all be citizens of the United States, and Spain will not have any voice whatever therein, which is proper, as no liability remains on her part.

It is to be hoped and trusted that there will not be the same delay in the adjudication and payment of claims existing against Spain at the present time in favor of our citizens, as happened in the cases of French spoliation, and Spanish-Florida claims; as to the former, some of them still remain unsettled. Many of them were not settled until more than three-quarters of a century had elapsed since Louisiana had been ceded partly in payment therefor.

ARTICLE VIII.

In fulfillment of articles 1, 2 and 3 of this treaty Spain renounces in Cuba, and cedes in Porto Rico and the other West Indian isles, in Guam and the Philippine archipelago, all buildings, moles, barracks, fortresses, establishments, public roads and other real property, which by custom or right are of the public domain, and as such belong to the crown of Spain. Nevertheless, it is declared that this renouncement or cession, as the case may be, referred to in the previous paragraph, in no way lessens the property or rights which belong by custom or law to the peaceful possessor of goods of all kinds in the provinces and cities, public or private establishments, civil or ecclesiastical, corporations or whatever bodies have judicial personality to acquire and possess goods in the above mentioned renounced or ceded territories, and those of private individuals, whatever be their nationality. The said renouncement or cession includes all those documents which exclusively refer to said renounced or ceded sovereignty which exist in the archives of the peninsula. When these documents existing in said archives only in part refer to said sovereignty, copies of said part shall be supplied, provided they be requested. Similar rules are to be reciprocally observed in favor of Spain with respect to the documents existing in the archives of the before mentioned islands. In the above mentioned renunciation or cession are comprised the rights of the crown of Spain and of its authorities over the archives and official registers, administrative and judicial, of said islands which refer to them and to the rights and properties of their inhabitants. Said archives and registers must be carefully preserved and all individuals, without exception, shall have the right to obtain, conformably to law, authorized copies of contracts, wills and other documents which form part of notarial protocols or which are kept in administrative and judicial archives, whether the same be in Spain or in the islands above mentioned.

Transfer of Public Property.—This is the usual clause by which a ceding nation vests in the acquiring government the public property. Whatever belonged to the Crown in Porto Rico, the Philippines and Guam, will now vest absolutely in the United States, and, as from the sale of public lands in Florida, Louisiana, California and the other acquired territories, the United States realized hundreds of millions of dollars, so from the uncultivated and unoccupied lands of these vast territories, the United States will be able to realize in part, if not, as is likely, in whole, or even possibly with an excess, the expenditure which the acquisition of these territories has involved.

In all of the prior cases of cessions, commissions were appointed by which the public domain was ascertained, and rights of private owners established, and due regard was given to the rights of all private citizens, but no claims were allowed as to ownership of unoccupied territory that were not clearly proved, and which would not have been equally valid as to land within our own territory. In this respect, however, the Supreme Court has decided in a long series of cases, known as the French and Spanish land cases, that whatever would have been a good title had the land remained under the prior sovereign, would be recognized after the acquisition, with the exception that the United States had a right to make, as it did, a limitation as to area.

In this respect see Act of March 3, 1891, entitled, "An Act to

Establish a Court of Private Land Claims, and to Provide for the
Settlement of Private Land Claims in Certain States and Territories," which was a general act passed by Congress so as to cover
all of the numerous cases involving claims of individuals
for property in the various States and Territories, and which are
based upon foreign grants, deeds, and other modes of obtaining
title, other than regular recorded transfer and actual occupation.

See also Reynolds on Mexican and Spanish Claims, in which
all of the law and most of the cases on these subjects have been
carefully collated.

Private Rights.—The second clause of Article VIII protects
the private rights of the peaceful possession of goods of all kinds,
both individual and corporate, and it is merely an expression in
the treaty of what has been decided to be the established law by
the Supreme Court, in the cases affecting cession of territory and
change of sovereignty. The principal cases in the United States
Supreme Court affecting the construction of treaties, so far as the
rights of inhabitants and owners are concerned, arising from a
change of sovereignty, are: *Foster* v. *Neilson*, 2 Peters 253;
Harcourt v. *Gailiard*, 12 Wheaton, 523; *Garcia* v. *Lee*, 12 Peters, 511, p. 517. The rule is expressed in two cases in the Supreme Court as follows:

> Even in cases of conquest, it is very unusual for the con-
> queror to do more than to displace the sovereign and assume
> dominion over the country. The modern usage of nations,
> which has become law, would be violated; that sense of jus-
> tice and of right, which is acknowledged and felt by the
> whole civilized world, would be outraged, if private prop-
> erty should be generally confiscated, and private rights an-
> nulled on a change of the sovereignty of the country, by the
> Florida treaty. The people change their allegiance, their
> relation to their ancient sovereign is dissolved; but their re-
> lations to each other and their rights of property remain un-
> disturbed. Had Florida changed its sovereign by an act
> containing no stipulation respecting the property of indi-
> viduals, the rights of property in all those who became sub-
> jects of citizens of the new government would have been un-
> affected by the change. It would have remained the same

as under the ancient sovereign. *U. S. v. Percheman*, 7 Peters, 51.

"By the law of nations, the inhabitants, citizens, or subjects of a conquered or ceded country, territory or province, retain all the rights of property which have not been taken from them by the orders of the conquerer; and this is the rule by which we must test its efficacy according to the act of Congress, which we must consider as of binding authority.

A treaty of cession is a deed or grant by one sovereign to another, which transferred nothing to which he had no right of property; and only such right as he owned, and could convey to the grantee. By the treaty with Spain the United States acquired no lands in Florida to which any person had lawfully obtained such a right by a perfect or inchoate title, and which this court could consider as property under the second article; or which had, according to the stipulations of the eighth article of the treaty, been granted by the lawful authorities of the king; which words, grants, or concessions, were to be construed in their broadest sense, so as to comprehend all lawful acts which operated to transfer a right of property, perfect or imperfect.— *U. S. v. Clark*, 9 Peters, 168.

From these decisions it appears that the rights of private individuals under the modern and civilized rules of warfare are not affected by change of sovereignty, and while the treaty does not say that *bona fide* claims of citizens of one country against citizens of the other shall be protected, this sentence would seem to certainly create the inference that it was not intended in any way that the old rules of war, which resulted in the cancellation of such debts, should apply at the present time. In fact, the theory of the present treaty seems to be that peace having been restored, commercial relations between the countries and between the citizens will be restored to their former status. See note also on this subject after Article XVIII.

Books and Archives.—This clause of Article VIII is very important. It has not infrequently happened that books and archives have been taken away by the ceding power, and that thereafter it has been practically impossible to adjust the claims and establish the rights of citizens, and great trouble and expense has resulted from such action. As to Florida, for instance, it required a special commission to examine the archives in Cuba and in Spain, to ascertain the condition of the titles.

The provision for copying and transmitting archives, and affording reciprocal courtesies in this respect, will also save a vast amount of trouble in adjusting titles and property rights. .

Renunciation and Cession of Sovereignty.—This clause is evidently put in to avoid any questions relating to the administrative functions of the new government, and of vesting the inchoate and intangible rights of sovereignty in the new government, as well as the actual ownership of property.

While it might be considered as an inseparable appurtenant, still the expression in the treaty is a wise precaution so to avoid any question in that regard.

Copies of Documents.—The final clause of Article VIII, giving an absolute right to parties interested to obtain copies of documents, is also a wise provision, and will save a great deal of diplomatic correspondence, and puts every person interested, from a property point of view, in the position of being able to prove his claim, if he has any.

ARTICLE IX.

Spanish subjects, natives of the peninsula, dwelling in the territory whose sovereignty Spain renounces or cedes in the present treaty, may remain in said territory or leave it, maintaining in one or the other case all their rights of property, including the right to sell and dispose of said property or its products, and moreover, they shall retain the right to exercise their industry, business or profession, submitting themselves in this respect to the laws which are applicable to other foreigners. In case they remain in the territory they may preserve their Spanish nationality by making in a registry office within a year after the interchange of the ratifications of this treaty, a declaration of their intention to preserve said nationality. Failing in this declaration they will be considered as having renounced said nationality and as having adopted that of the

*erritory in which they may reside. The civil rights and political
status of the native inhabitants of the territories hereby ceded to the
United States shall be determined by Congress.*

Article IX, relating, as it does, to the rights of citizenship, and
the civil and political status of the inhabitants of the ceded
territory, is one of the most important articles of the treaty. Ap
parently the Commissioners have covered every possible question
that could arise. They have adhered to the established rules and
customs of treaty expressions, as adopted and exercised by the
United States, but at the same time have so modified them that
the constitutional questions which will necessarily arise, as to the
rights of the eleven million inhabitants (or thereabouts) of the
ceded territory, can undoubtedly be disposed of by the precedents
already established.

The unlimited power of Congress to govern territory belong
ing to the United States has been established in a long series of
decisions by the Supreme Court, but the status of the inhabitants,
in the absence of special treaty stipulations, might have been con
trolled by that part of the 14th amendment, which relates to
citizenship (see Appendix); but the decisions of the Supreme
Court and the opinions of the leading publicists are all to the ef
fect that stipulations in a treaty of cession are paramount in es
tablishing the status of the inhabitants. In this respect Story
says (Sec. 1328):

"The power of Congress over the whole territory is clearly
exclusive and universal, and their legislation is subject to
no control, but is absolute and unlimited, unless so far as af
fected by stipulations in the cession or by the ordinance of
1887, in which any part of it has been settled."

The principal cases in the Supreme Court on this subject are:
American Ins. Co. vs. Canter, 1 Peters, 511; *Mormon Church
case,* 136 U. S., 1; *Bank vs. Yankton,* 101 U. S., 129; *Murphy
vs. Ramsey,* 114 U. S., 15; *Jones vs. U. S.,* 137 U. S., 202.

Rawle (Edition of 1829, page 237) says, that Congress has al
ways been entitled to regulate the form of government of terri
tories subject only to treaty stipulations.

In that respect the treaty stipulations are paramount to all Constitutional provisions, and, in fact, it can be stated as a rule of law, that treaty stipulations are the only limitations by which Congress would be limited in establishing the status of the inhabitants.

The last clause of Article IX places the entire power in the hands of Congress, and, therefore, the inhabitants of the ceded territory have no greater rights, under the cession by which they pass under the jurisdiction of the United States, than Congress shall confer upon them.

The provisions according privileges to the inhabitants, however, correspond with similar provisions in the prior treaties.

Article III of the Louisiana Treaty (U. S. Treaty Volume, Page 332) provided:

"That the inhabitants of the ceded territory shall be incorporated in the union of the United States, and admitted as soon as possible according to the principles of the Federal Constitution to the enjoyment of all the rights, advantages and immunities of the citizens of the United States, and in the meantime they shall be maintained and protected in the free enjoyment of their liberty, property, and the religion which they profess."

Articles V and VI of the treaty of 1819 with Spain for the cession of Florida (U. S. Treaty, Volume, Page 1018) are:

V. The inhabitants of the ceded territories shall be secured in the free exercise of their religion without any restriction, and all those who may desire to remove to the Spanish dominions shall be permitted to sell or export their effects at any time whatever, without being subject in either case to duties.

VI. The inhabitants of the territories which His Catholic Majesty cedes to the United States by this treaty shall be incorporated in the union of the United States, as soon as may be consistent with the principles of the Federal Constitution, and admitted to the enjoyment of all privileges, rights and immunities of citizens of the United States."

The treaty of Guadaloupe-Hidalgo (U. S. Treaty, Volume, Page 684) provided:

Article VIII.—Mexicans now established in territories

previously belonging to Mexico, and which remain for the future within the limits of the United States, defined by the present shall be free to continue where they now reside, or to remove at any time to the Mexican Republic, retaining the property which they possess in the said territories, or disposing thereof, and removing the proceeds wherever they please, without their being subjected, on this account, to any contribution, tax, or charge whatever.

Those who shall prefer to remain in the said territories may either retain the title and rights of Mexican citizens, or acquire those of citizens of the United States. But they shall be under the obligation to make their election within one year from the date of the exchange of ratifications of this treaty; and those who shall remain in the said territories after the expiration of that year, without having declared their intention to retain the character of Mexicans, shall be considered to have elected to become citizens of the United States.

In the said territories, property of every kind, now belonging to Mexicans not established there, shall be inviolably respected. The present owners, the heirs of these, and all Mexicans who may hereafter acquire said property by contract, shall enjoy with respect to it guarantees equally ample as if the same belonged to citizens of the United States.

Article IX. The Mexicans who, in the territories aforesaid, shall not preserve the character of citizens of the Mexican Republic, conformably with what is stipulated in the preceding article, shall be incorporated into the union of the United States, and be admitted at the proper time (to be judged by the Congress of the United States) to the enjoyment of all the rights of citizens of the United States, according to the principles of the Constitution; and in the meantime, shall be maintained and protected in the free enjoyment of their liberty and property, and secured in the free exercise of their religion without restriction.

The Gadsden-Mexican treaty of 1853 (U. S. Treaty, Volume, page 696) provided, "that all the provisions of the two articles of the Guadaloupe-Hidalgo treaty just quoted, and that the same articles should also apply to all the rights of persons and property, both civil and ecclesiastical, within the same.

as fully and as effectually as if the said articles were herein
again recited and set forth."

Article III of the Russian Treaty of 1867 (U. S. Treaty, Volume, 941) is as follows:

"The inhabitants of the ceded territory, according to their
choice, reserving their national allegiance, may return to
Russia within three years; but if they should prefer to remain in the ceded territory, they, with the exception of uncivilized native tribes, shall be admitted to the enjoyment
of all the rights, advantages and immunities of citizens of
the United States, and shall be maintained and protected
in the free enjoyment of their liberty, property and religion.
The uncivilized tribes shall be subject to such laws and regulations as the United States may from time to time adopt,
in regard to aboriginal tribes of that country." The Fourteenth Amendment had been adopted by Congress and was
before the States for ratification when this treaty was concluded.

Texas was not annexed by treaty. A treaty was proposed to
the Senate, and failed. It required two-thirds of the Senate.
A majority of both houses of Congress united, however, in a
joint resolution, March 1, 1845 (See U. S. Statutes at Large),
which specified the terms upon which Texas became a State of
the Union.

Hawaii was also annexed by the United States after a treaty
had failed, by joint resolution (See Appendix), the differ-
ence between the annexation of Texas and that of Hawaii being, that in the former instance Texas was admitted as a State while Hawaii was admitted only as
a Territory; but in both cases the joint resolution contained limitations as to the status and rights of the inhabitants.
In the case of Texas, slavery was prohibited north of 36.30, the
line of the Missouri Compromise, and in the Hawaiian case the
resolution provides: "There shall be no further immigration of
Chinese in the Hawaiian Islands, except upon such conditions as are now, or may hereafter be, allowed by the laws
of the United States; and no Chinese, by reason of anything
heretofore contained, shall be allowed to enter the United
States from the Hawaiian Islands."

The record of the United States Government, from the earliest acquisition of territory, has been to control the status of inhabitants in newly acquired territory, by the terms of the cession, and all privileges and immunities acquired as a matter of right have been only those that have been given under the terms of the treaty of cession.

ARTICLE X.

The inhabitants of the territories whose sovereignty Spain renounces or cedes shall have assured to them the free exercise of their religion.

Guaranty of Religious Freedom.—The notes and excerpts from the various treaties, under Article IX, apply equally to the guaranty of free exercise of religion by the inhabitants of the ceded territory, except that under this paragraph the United States apparently assumes the protection of worshippers in the Island of Cuba, and they have this right by virtue of the supreme power given to the President as Commander-in-Chief, under the rules of military occupancy.

ARTICLE XI.

Spaniards residing in the territories whose Sovereignty Spain cedes or renounces shall be subject in civil and criminal matters to the tribunals of the country in which they reside, conformably with the common laws which regulate their competence, being enabled to appear before them in the same manner and to employ the same proceedings as the citizens of the country to which the tribunal belongs must observe.

Status of Spanish Subjects.—By this article, citizens of Spain or inhabitants of Spanish descent, who choose to remain in the territory after the cession, while they must subject themselves to the same laws which control the inhabitants who become citizens, or who remain there subject to such rules and regulations as Congress may prescribe, will still be entitled to all the privileges and immunities which those inhabitants are accorded by the United States.

It can hardly be conceived that the United States would deny to any of the inhabitants of Spain any of those privileges, and the clause simply makes a corresponding obligation to conform to the laws, in the consideration of the equal privileges accorded.

ARTICLE XII.

Judicial proceedings pending on the interchange of the ratifications of this treaty in the territories over which Spain renounces or cedes sovereignty shall be determined conformably with the following rules:

FIRST—Sentences pronounced in civil cases between individuals or in criminal cases before the above-mentioned date, and against which there is no appeal or annulment conformably with the Spanish law, shall be considered as lasting, and shall be executed in due form by competent authority in the territory within which said sentences should be carried out.

SECOND—Civil actions between individuals, which on the afore mentioned date have not been decided, shall continue their course before the tribunal in which the lawsuit is proceeding, or before that which shall replace it.

THIRD.—Criminal actions pending on the afore-mentioned date before the supreme tribunal of Spain against citizens of territory, which, according to this treaty, will cease to be Spanish, shall continue under its jurisdiction until definite sentence is pronounced, but once sentence is decreed its execution shall be intrusted to competent authority of the place where the action arises.

Conduct of Judicial Proceedings.—By this article the conduct of civil and criminal actions pending in the ceded territories will not be interrupted by a change of sovereignty. Honest creditors will not be deprived of their remedies, and delinquent debtors and criminals will not be able to avail of the change, in order either to avoid payment of just debts, or escape punishment for their crimes.

This article is in accord with the accepted rule of International Law, that change of sovereignty should not exercise any effect on local or personal interests. This is a rule which has been pronounced and sustained by the Supreme Court of the United States as a natural rule of law, and one that proceeds from a just interpretation of the mutual rights as between nations, as well as between the citizens of different nations and the governing powers. See notes under Article VIII and cases there cited.

ARTICLE XIII.

Literary, artistic, and industrial rights of property acquired by Spaniards in Cuba, Porto Rico, the Philippines and other territories ceded on the interchange of ratifications of this treaty, shall continue to be respected. Spanish scientific, literary, and artistic works not dangerous to public order in said territories, shall continue entering therein with freedom from all custom duties for a period of ten years dating from the interchange of the ratifications of this treaty.

Works of Art.—This article is another evidence of the progress of the civilization upon international relations, resulting from the advance of the arts and science; while in this instance, the results of science, literature and art are exempted from tariff charges for a period of ten years, the right of entry, and the exemption of duty, are both properly limited, so that they can not be available of for any detrimental or improper purposes; as there is no limitation as to the right of adjudication, it remains absolutely within the power of the Government of the territory—the United States—to determine to what extent the right of exclusion, on the ground of danger to public order, shall be exercised.

ARTICLE XIV.

Spain may establish consular agents in the ports and places of the territories whose renunciation or cession are the object of this treaty.

Consular Representation.—This is a positive recognition by treaty of a right which would doubtless have been accorded to Spain, whether any reference was made thereto in the treaty or not, as it has always been the custom of the United States not only to grant, but to invite, consular representation in our territory by all foreign nations.

The article further undoubtedly presages a renewal of not only of all consular, but also of diplomatic relations between the two countries, which so lately have been at war with each other, and the sooner those relations are established, and all memory of hostilities effaced, the better it will be for both nations, and all of the inhabitants thereof.

ARTICLE XV.

The government of either country shall concede for a term of ten years to the merchant ships of the other the same treatment as regards all port dues, including those of entry and departure, lighthouse and tonnage dues, as it concedes to its own merchant ships not employed in the coasting trade. This article may be repudiated at any time by either government giving previous notice thereof six months beforehand.

The notes under Article IV are to some extent also applicable to this article, except that the privileges in Article XV can be cancelled, and the article repudiated at any time by either Government, on giving six months notice; this article, however, relates not only to the privileges which are to be accorded to Spanish vessels in ports which have now become Americanized, but also to the vessels of the United States in ports that remain under the control of Spain.

The right to repudiate may or may not be exercised, but there are several instances in which a similar right of repudiation has not been exercised for many years.

The agreement of 1817 with Great Britain as to the use and construction of naval vessels on the Great Lakes, and which has resulted in the complete disarmament of those great inland oceans, has a similar clause for termination on six months notice, but it has been in effect uninterruptedly for eighty-one years.

ARTICLE XVI.

Be it understood that whatever obligations are accepted under this treaty by the United States with respect to Cuba are limited to the period of their occupation of the island, but at the end of said occupation they will advise the government that may be established in the island that it should accept the same obligations.

Obligations of Cuban Occupancy; New Government.—The obligations imposed upon this Government, by reason of its military occupancy of the Island of Cuba, have been discussed at length under Article I, and will not be again referred to here.

Article XVI definitely settles that the United States does not assume any permanent responsibilities under this treaty, as to Cuba, but only the obligations growing out of the fact that during the period of occupancy they will be bound to maintain law and order in the occupied territory. The provision that, at the end of the occupation, they will advise such government as may be established in the island that it should accept the same obligations, does not create any positive obligation to obtain any such assumption. But it will unquestionably be the duty of the United States not to surrender the military control over Cuba until satisfactory assurances are given that the obligations of maintaining law and order, will not only be assumed by some government, but will be assumed by a government able to fulfil them; in this connection it must be noted that none of these obligations in any way relate to an assumption of debt, for, as a matter of fact, they are exclusively confined to those obligations that are currently created by the exercise of sovereignty over the territory, and not by virtue of any purchase or acquisition of territory entailing the assumption of debt.

ARTICLE XVII.

The present treaty shall be ratified by the Queen Regent of Spain and the President of the United States, in agreement and with the approval of the Senate, and ratifications shall be exchanged in Washington within a delay of six months from this date, or earlier if possible.

The exchange of ratifications is always provided for in the final articles of treaties, and the time within which the exchange shall take place definitely fixed. Ratification is always necessary in the case of a treaty concluded on behalf of the United States, and the powers given to Commissioners always refer to this requirement, which, as already stated, is constitutional. (See Appendix.)

It has not infrequently happened that treaties concluded by Commissioners have failed to meet the approbation of a two-thirds majority of the Senate; this happened, amongst other instances, in the following cases: Treaty for Annexation of Texas; treaty for Annexation of San Domingo, 1870; treaty for Annexation of Hawaii; Bayard-Chamberlain fisheries treaty, 1888; the treaty of peace in 1848, with Mexico, was not accepted, as a whole as it came from the Commissioners, but was conditionally ratified with certain amendments and omissions, subject to acceptance by Mexico, and when Mexico accepted the changes, the treaty became operative.

Commercial Intercourse; Diplomatic Relations.— In the text of the treaty nothing whatever appears as to revival of commercial intercourse and diplomatic relations between the two Governments. Possibly something appears in the preamble, but the text as cabled omits all the formal preambles, and those statements which usually precede the first article of a treaty, and which often determine the nature of the instrument for the purpose of its construction.

It is still a mooted question in International Law whether or not a treaty of peace revives existing treaties, without a special provision to that effect. In this respect the protocols showing the intention of the Commissioners may have an important bearing upon the subject.

According to Woolsey (N. Y. 1897, page 263):

"Although a peace is a return to a state of amity, and among civilized nations, of intercourse, the conditions on which intercourse is adopted may not be the same as before the war. If a treaty contain no other agreement than that there should be peace between the parties, there would be a fair presumption that everything was settled again on its old basis, the cause of war alone being still unsettled. But treaties usually define anew the terms of intercourse; the general principles which govern the renewal of intercourse can not be laid down until it is first known what the effect of a war is upon previous treaties."

The English rule has been that all treaties are suspended, and must be revived, and that was the position which the British Commissioners took with our Commissioners when the treaty of Ghent was negotiated—the conclusion of which, by the way, bears an interesting similarity to the present treaty, in that the treaty of peace that terminated the war of 1812 was concluded on Christmas Eve, 1814, and the treaty in the present instance will be handed on the same anniversary day in 1898, to the Executive by whom the Commissioners were appointed.

The rule then laid down by the British Commissioners, and which has always since been disputed by American authorities, was that the war had terminated all commercial treaties and privileges, and that they were not revived by the treaty, in the absence of a special stipulation.

The legal question has never really been decided, and Woolsey, on the same page above cited, asks the question, "But does war end all treaties?" and discusses it at length in a way that shows it is still an open question.

The practical effect in 1814 was that the United States lost the right of the inshore fisheries off the North Atlantic Provinces, and Great Britain lost the right of the internal navigation of the Mississippi.

Glenn states it on page 259, as follows:

"A treaty of peace puts an end to all quarrels which resulted in the war that has just been waged, whether expressly mentioned or not. It renders operative and binding certain treaties or international agreements, the operation of which has been suspended by the war."

And he cites as authorities of the existing rule, Hall's International Law, page 561-562; 3 Phillmore, Section 524 et. seq.; Calvo's International Law, Sections 3155-3159.

This question is one, however, of minor importance, as the commercial relations between the two countries will have to be reinstated on a new basis, the commercial treaty in force when war was declared being the original treaty, negotiated in 1759, and which will need thorough overhauling in any event.

The effect of peace, however, on the private relations of citizens of the two countries lately at war, as between each other, is definitely settled.

It was formerly considered necessary to make some special stipulation in this respect, as was done in the Treaty of Peace with Great Britain, in 1783, but the generally adopted theory is now expressed by Glenn on pages 259, section 216:

> "Private rights, the right of prosecution of which is suspended by the war, are revived by the peace, even though nothing be said upon the subject in the treaty."

Hall has summarized the whole matter in the third clause of section 200, page 584, of his fourth edition:

> "3. In a general way, peace revives all private rights, and restores the remedies which have been suspended during the war; contracts, for example, are revived between private persons, if they are not of such a kind as to be necessarily put an end to by war, and if their fulfillment has not been rendered impossible by such acts of a belligerent government, as the confiscation of debts due the subjects to those of its enemy; the courts also are reopened for the enforcement of claims of every kind."

In this respect Woolsey says, on page 265:

> "But private rights, the prosecution of which is interrupted by war, are revived by peace, although nothing be said upon the subject; for a peace is a return to a normal state of things, and private rights depend not so much on concessions, like public ones, as on common views of justice. And this includes not only claims of private persons, in the two countries, upon one another, but also claims of individuals on the government of the foreign country, and claims—private and not political—of each government upon the other existing before the war." The treaty provisions, however, in this case will control as to claims against either government. (See notes under Article VII.)

The Supreme Court of the United States passed upon this question in 1867, and in the case of *Hanger* v. *Abbott*, 6 Wall. 532, decided that the "old decissions made when the rule of law was that war annulled all debts between the subjects of the belligerents, are entitled to but little weight, even if it is safe to assume that they are correctly reported, of which, in respect to the leading case, there is much doubt.

"All of those decisions were made between parties who were citizens of the same jurisdiction, and most of them were made nearly one hundred years before the international rule was acknowledged, that war only suspended debts due to an enemy, and that peace had the effect to restore the remedy. The rule of the present day is that debts existing prior to the war, but which made no part of the reasons for undertaking it, remain entire, and the remedies are revived at the restoration of peace."

In the same case it was also decided that during the period of the war the statute of limitations does not run. There does not seem to be any decision during which the exact period of hostilities is defined as to the statute of limitations.

Probably the period of suspension would commence with the declaration of war, and would not terminate until the treaty of peace was actually made, and the ratifications exchanged, as there would be no renewel of commercial right; and probably no citizen of one nation would have any standing in the courts of the other until that event transpired.

Numerous legal questions which will arise both under Constitutional and International Law, in considering and constructing a treaty of peace as important as the one which has just been concluded, can not, of course, be disposed of in a brief pamphlet prepared without the inspection of the actual text, and without the opportunity for extended research and examination of all of the numerous historical and legal precedents affecting it, and the foregoing brief statement is only intended to be used as a guide to direct those desiring to examine the subject, to the sources whence greater information may be obtained.

APPENDIX.

EXTRACTS FROM CONSTITUTION OF THE UNITED STATES.

We, the people of the United States, in order to form a more perfect Union, establish justice, insure domestic tranquility, provide for the common defence, promote the general welfare, and secure the blessings of liberty to ourselves and our posterity, do ordain and establish this Constitution for the United States of America.

Article 1, Section 1. All legislative powers herein granted shall be vested in a Congress of the United States, which shall consist of a Senate and House of Representatives.

Article 1, Section 8. The Congress shall have power to lay and collect taxes, duties, imposts and excises, to pay the debts and provide for the common defence and general welfare of the United States; but all duties, imposts and excises shall be uniform throughout the United States.

To borrow money on the credit of the United States.

To regulate commerce with foreign nations, and among the several States, and with the Indian tribes.

To establish an uniform rule of naturalization, and uniform laws on the subject of bankruptcies throughout the United States.

To coin money, regulate the value thereof, and of foreign coin, and fix the standard of weights and measures.

To provide for the punishment of counterfeiting the securities and current coin of the United States.

To establish postoffices and post roads.

To promote the progress of science and useful arts, by securing for limited times to authors and inventors the exclusive right to their respective writings and discoveries.

To constitute tribunals inferior to the Supreme Court.

To define and punish piracies and felonies committed on the high seas, and offences against the law of nations.

To declare war, grant letters of marque and reprisal, and make rules concerning captures on land and water.

To raise and support armies, but no appropriation of money to that use shall be for a longer term than two years.

To provide and maintain a navy.

To make rules for the government and regulation of the land and naval forces.

To provide for calling forth the militia to execute the laws of the Union, suppress insurrections and repel invasions.

To provide for organizing, arming and disciplining the militia, and for governing such part of them as may be employed in the service of the United States, reserving to the States, respectively, the appointment of the officers, and the authority of training the militia according to the discipline prescribed by Congress.

To exercise exclusive legislation in all cases whatsoever, over such District (not exceeding ten miles square) as may, by cession of particular States, and the acceptance of Congress, become the seat of the Government of the United States, and to exercise like authority over all places purchased by the consent of the legislature of the State in which the same shall be, for the erection of forts, magazines, arsenals, dock yards, and other needful buildings; and

To make all laws which shall be necessary and proper for carrying into execution the foregoing powers, and all other powers vested by this Constitution in the Government of the United States, or in any Department or officer thereof.

Section 10. No State shall enter into any treaty, alliance or confederation; grant letters of marque and reprisal; coin money; emit bills of credit; make anything but gold and silver coin a tender in payment of debts; pass any bill of attainder, ex post facto law, or law impairing the obligation of contracts, or grant any title of nobility.

No State shall, without the consent of the Congress, lay any imposts or duties on imports or exports, except what may be absolutely necessary for executing it's inspection laws; and the net produce of all duties and imposts, laid by any State on imports or exports, shall be for the use of the Treasury of the United States; and all such laws shall be subject to the revision and control of the Congress.

No State shall, without the consent of Congress, lay any duty of tonnage, keep troops or ships or war in time of peace, enter into any agreement or compact with another State, or with a foreign power, or engage in war, unless actually invaded, or in such imminent danger as will not admit of delay.

Article II, Section 1. The executive power shall be vested in a President of the United States of America. He shall hold his office during the term of four years, and, together with the Vice-President, chosen for the same term, be elected as follows:

Article II, Section 2. The President shall be Commander-in-Chief of the Army and Navy of the United States, and of the militia of the several States, when called into the actual service of the United States; he may require the opinion, in writing, of the principal officer in each of the Executive Departments, upon any subject relating to the duties of their respective offices, and he shall have power to grant reprieves and pardons for offences against the United States, except in cases of impeachment.

He shall have power, by and with the advice and consent of the Senate, to make treaties, provided two-thirds of the Senators present concur; and he shall nominate, and by and with the advice and consent of the Senate, shall appoint Ambassadors, other public ministers and consuls, judges of the Supreme Court, and all other officers of the United States, whose appointments are not herein otherwise provided for, and which shall be established by law; but the Congress may by law vest the appointment of such inferior officers, as they think proper, in the President alone, in the courts of law, or in the heads of Departments.

The President shall have power to fill up all vacancies that may happen during the recess of the Senate, by granting commissions which shall expire at the end of their next session.

Section 3. He shall from time to time give to the Congress information of the state of the Union, and recommend to their consideration such measures as he shall judge necessary and expedient; he may, on extraordinary occasions, convene both Houses, or either of them, and in case of disagreement between them, with respect to the time of adjournment, he may adjourn them to such time as he shall think proper; he shall receive Ambassadors and other public Ministers; he shall take care that the laws be faithfully executed, and shall commission all the officers of the United States.

Article IV. Section 3. New States may be admitted by the Congress into this Union, but no new State shall be formed or erected within the jurisdiction of any other State, nor any State be formed by the junction of two or more States, or parts of States, without the consent of the legislatures of the States concerned as well as of the Congress.

The Congress shall have power to dispose of and make all needful rules and regulations respecting the Territory or other property belonging to the United States; and nothing in this Constitution shall be so construed as to prejudice any claims of the United States, or of any particular State.

Section 4. The United States shall guarantee to every State in this Union a republican form of Government, and shall protect each of them against invasion; and on application of the legislature, or of the Executive (when the legislature can not be convened), against domestic violence.

Article V. The Congress, whenever two-thirds of both Houses shall deem it necessary, shall propose amendments to this Constitution, or, on the application of the legislatures of two-thirds of the several States, shall call a convention for proposing amendments, which, in either case, shall be valid to all intents and purposes, as part of this Constitution, when ratified by the legislatures of three-fourths of the several States, or by conventions in three-fourths thereof, as the one or the other mode of ratification may be proposed by the Congress. Provided, That no amendment which may be made prior to the year one thousand eight hundred and eight shall in any manner affect the first and fourth clauses in the Ninth Section of the First Article, and that no State, without its consent, shall be deprived of its equal suffrage in the Senate.

Article VI. All debts contracted and engagements entered into, before the adoption of this Constitution, shall be as valid against the United States under this Constitution, as under the Confederation.

This Constitution, and the laws of the United States which shall be made in pursuance thereof, and all treaties made, or which shall be made, under the authority of the United States, shall be the supreme law of the land, and the judges in every State shall be bound thereby, anything in the constitution or laws of any State to the contrary notwithstanding.

The Senators and Representatives before mentioned, and the members of the several State legislatures, and all executive and judicial officers, both of the United States and of the several States, shall be bound by oath or affirmation, to support this Constitution; but no religious test shall ever be required as a qualification to any office or public trust under the United States.

First Amendment. Congress shall make no law respecting an establishment of religion, or prohibiting the free exercise thereof; or abridging the freedom of speech, or of the press; or of the right of the people peaceably to assemble, and to petition the Government for a redress of grievances.

Ninth Amendment. The enumeration, in the Constitution, of certain rights, shall not be construed to deny or disparage others retained by the people.

Tenth Amendment. The powers not delegated to the United States by the Constitution, nor prohibited by it to the States, are reserved to the States respectively, or to the people.

Thirteenth Amendment. Section 1. Neither slavery nor involuntary servitude, except as a punishment for crime whereof the party shall have been duly convicted, shall exist within the United States, or any place subject to their jurisdiction.

Fourteenth Amendment. Section 1. All persons born or naturalized in the United States, and subject to the jurisdiction thereof, are citizens of the United States and of the State wherein they reside. No State shall make or enforce any law which shall abridge the privileges or immunities of citizens of the United States; nor shall any State deprive any person of life, liberty or property without due process of law; nor deny to any person within its jurisdiction the equal protection of the laws.

Fifteenth Amendment. Section 1. The right of citizens of the United States to vote shall not be denied or abridged by the United States or by any State on account of race, color or previous condition of servitude.

30 U. S. STATUTES AT LARGE, 750—PUBLIC RESOLUTION, NO. 51, JULY 7, 1898.

JOINT RESOLUTION TO PROVIDE FOR ANNEXING THE HAWAIIAN ISLANDS TO THE UNITED STATES.

Whereas, the government of the Republic of Hawaii having, in due form, signified its consent, in the manner provided by its constitution, to cede absolutely and without reserve to the United States of America all rights of sovereignty of whatsoever kind in and over the Hawaiian Islands and their dependencies, and also to cede and transfer to the United States the absolute fee and ownership of all public, government, or crown lands, public buildings or edifices, ports, harbors, military equipment, and all other public property of every kind and description belonging to the government of the Hawaiian Islands, together with every right and appurtenance thereunto appertaining: Therefore,

Resolved by the Senate and House of Representatives of the United States of America in Congress assembled, That said cession is accepted, ratified and confirmed, and that the said Hawaiian Islands and their dependencies be, and they are hereby, annexed as a part of the territory of the United States and are subject to the sovereign dominion thereof, and that all and singular the property and rights hereinbefore mentioned are vested in the United States of America.

The existing laws of the United States relative to public lands shall not apply to such lands in the Hawaiian Islands; but the Congress of the United States shall enact special laws for their management and disposition: Provided, That all revenue from or proceeds of the same, except as regards such part thereof as may be used or occupied for the civil, military or naval purposes of the United States, or may be assigned for the use of the local government, shall be used, solely for the benefit of the inhabitants of the Hawaiian Islands for educational and other public purposes.

Until Congress shall provide for the government of such islands all the civil, judicial and military powers exercised by the officers of the existing government in said islands shall be vested in such person or persons and shall be exercised in such manner as the President of the United States shall direct; and the President shall have power to remove said officers and fill the vacancies so occasioned.

The existing treaties of the Hawaiian Islands with foreign nations shall forthwith cease and determine, being replaced by such treaties as may exist, or as may be hereafter concluded, between the United States and such foreign nations. The municipal legislation of the Hawaiian Islands, not enacted for the fulfillment of the treaties so extinguished, and not inconsistent with this joint resolution nor contrary to the Constitution of the United States nor to any existing treaty of the United States, shall remain in force until the Congress of the United States shall otherwise determine.

Until legislation shall be enacted extending the United States customs laws and regulations to the Hawaiian Islands the existing customs relations of the Hawaiian Islands with the United States and other countries shall remain unchanged.

The public debt of the Republic of Hawaii, lawfully existing at the date of the passage of this joint resolution, including the amounts due to depositors in the Hawaiian Postal Savings Bank, is hereby assumed by the Government of the United States; but the liability of the United States in this regard shall in no case exceed four million dollars. So long, however, as the existing government and the present commercial relations of the Hawaiian Islands are continued as hereinbefore provided, said government shall continue to pay the interest on said debt.

There shall be no further immigration of Chinese into the Hawaiian Islands, except upon such conditions as are now or may hereafter be allowed by the laws of the United States; and no Chinese, by reason of anything herein contained, shall be allowed to enter the United States from the Hawaiian Islands.

The President shall appoint five commissioners, at least two of whom shall be residents of the Hawaiian Islands, who shall, as soon as reasonably practicable, recommend to Congress such legislation concerning the Hawaiian Islands as they shall deem necessary or proper.

Sec. 2. That the commissioners hereinbefore provided for shall be appointed by the President, by and with the advice and consent of the Senate.

Sec. 3. That the sum of one hundred thousand dollars, or so much thereof as may be necessary, is hereby appropriated, out of any money in the Treasury not otherwise appropriated, and to be immediately available, to be expended at the discretion of the President of the United States of America, for the purpose of carrying this joint resolution into effect.

Approved, July 7, 1898.

PROTOCOL.

William R. Day, Secretary of State of the United States, and His Excellency Jules Cambon, Ambassador Extraordinary and Plenipotentiary of the Republic of France, at Washington, respectively possessing for this purpose full authority from the Government of the United States and the government of Spain, have concluded and signed the following articles, embodying the terms on which the two governments have agreed in respect to the matters hereinafter set forth, having in view the establishment of peace between the two countries, that is to say:

ARTICLE 1.

Spain will relinquish all claim of sovereignty over and title to Cuba.

ARTICLE II.

Spain will cede to the United States the island of Porto Rico and other islands now under Spanish sovereignty in the West Indies, and also an island in the Ladrones to be selected by the United States.

ARTICLE III.

The United States will occupy and hold the city, bay and harbor of Manila, pending the conclusion of a treaty of peace which shall determine the control, disposition and government of the Philippines.

Spain will immediately evacuate Cuba, Porto Rico and other islands now under Spanish sovereignty in the West Indies; and to this end each government will, within ten days after the signing of this protocol, appoint Commissioners, and the Commissioners so appointed shall, within thirty days after the signing of this protocol, meet at Havana for the purpose of arranging and carrying out the details of the aforesaid evacuation of Cuba and the adjacent Spanish islands; and each government will, within ten days after the signing of this protocol, also appoint other Commissioners, who shall, within thirty days after the signing of this protocol, meet at San Juan, in Porto Rico, for the purpose of arranging and carrying out the details of the aforesaid evacuation of Porto Rico and other islands now under Spanish sovereignty in the West Indies.

ARTICLE V.

The United States and Spain will each appoint not more than five commissioners to treat of peace, and the commissioners so appointed shall meet at Paris not later than October 1, 1898, and proceed to the negotiation and conclusion of a treaty of peace, which treaty shall be subject to ratification according to the respective constitutional forms of the two countries.

ARTICLE VI.

Upon the conclusion and signing of this protocol, hostilities between the two countries shall be suspended, and notice to that effect shall be given as soon as possible by each government to the commanders of its military and naval forces.

Done at Washington in duplicate, in English and in French, by the undersigned, who have hereunto set their hands and seals, the 12th day of August, 1898.

|SEAL| WILLIAM R. DAY.
|SEAL| JULES CAMBON.

War Department, Adjutant-General's Office,
Washington, July 18, 1898.

The following, received from the President of the United States, is published for the information and guidance of all concerned:

Executive Mansion, Washington, July 13, 1898.
To the Secretary of War.

Sir: The capitulation of the Spanish forces in Santiago de Cuba and in the eastern part of the province of Santiago, and the occupation of the territory by the forces of the United States, render it necessary to instruct the military commander of the United States as to the conduct which he is to observe during the military occupation.

The first effect of the military occupation of the enemy's territory is the severance of the former political relations of the inhabitants, and the establishment of a new political power. Under this changed

condition of things, the inhabitants, so long as they perform their
duties, are entitled to security in their persons and property, and in
all their private rights and relations. It is my desire that the inhabitants of Cuba should be acquainted with the purpose of the United
States to discharge to the fullest extent its obligations in this regard.
It will, therefore, be the duty of the Commander of the army of occupation to announce and proclaim in the most public manner that we
come not to make war upon the inhabitants of Cuba, nor upon any
party or faction among them, but to protect them in their homes, in
their employments, and in their personal and religious rights. All
persons who, either by active aid or by honest submission, cooperate
with the United States in its efforts to give effect to this beneficent
purpose, will receive the reward of its support and protection. Our
occupation should be as free from severity as possible.

Though the powers of the military occupant are absolute and supreme, and immediately operate upon the political conditions of the
inhabitants, the municipal laws of the conquered territory, such as
affect private rights of person and property, and provide for the punishment of crime, are considered as continuing in force, so far as they
are compatible with the new order of things, until they are suspended
or superseded by the occupying belligerent; and in practice they are
not usually abrogated, but are allowed to remain in force, and to be
administered by the ordinary tribunals, substantially as they were
before the occupation. This enlightened practice is, so far as possible,
to be adhered to on the present occasion. The judges and the other
officials connected with the administration of justice may, if they
accept the supremacy of the United States, continue to administer the
ordinary law of the land, as between man and man, under the supervision of the American Commander-in-Chief. The native constabulary
will, so far as may be practicable, be preserved. The freedom of the
people to pursue their accustomed occupations will be abridged only
when it may be necessary to do so.

While the rule of conduct of the American Commander-in-Chief will
be such as has just been defined, it will be his duty to adopt measures
of a different kind, if, unfortunately, the course of the people should
render such measures indispensable to the maintenance of law and
order. He will then possess the power to replace or expel the native
officials in part or altogether, to substitute new courts of his own
constitution for those that now exist, or to create such new or sup-
plementary tribunals as may be necessary. In the exercise of these
high powers the commander must be guided by his judgment and his
experience, and a high sense of justice.

One of the most important and most practical problems with which
it will be necessary to deal is that of the treatment of property and
the collection and administration of the revenues. It is conceded that
all public funds and securities belonging to the government of the
country in its own right, and all arms and supplies and other movable
property of such government, may be seized by the military occupant
and converted to his own use. The real property of the state he may
hold and administer, at the same time enjoying the revenues thereof,
but he is not to destroy it save in the case of military necessity. All
public means of transportation, such as telegraph lines, cables, railways and boats belonging to the state, may be appropriated to his use,
but, unless in case of military necessity, they are not to be destroyed.
All churches and buildings devoted to religious worship and to the
arts and sciences and all schoolhouses are, so far as possible to be
protected; and all destruction or intentional defacement of such

places, of historical monuments or archives or of works of science or art is prohibited, save when required by urgent military necessity.

Private property, whether belonging to individuals or corporations, is to be respected, and can be confiscated only for cause. Means of transportation, such as telegraph lines and cables, railways and boats may, although they belong to private individuals or corporations, be seized by the military occupant, but unless destroyed under military necessity, are not to be retained.

While it is held to be the right of the conqueror to levy contributions upon the enemy in their seaports, towns or provinces which may be in his military possession by conquest, and to apply the proceeds to defray the expenses of the war, this right is to be exercised within such limitations that it may not savor of confiscation. As the result of military occupation the taxes and duties payable by the inhabitants to the former government become payable to the military occupant, unless he sees fit to substitute for them other rates or modes of contribution to the expenses of the government. The monies so collected are to be used for the purpose of paying the expenses of government under the military occupation, such as the salaries of the judges and the police, and for the payment of the expenses of the army.

Private property taken for the use of the army is to be paid for when possible in cash at a fair valuation, and when payment in cash is not possible, receipts are to be given.

All ports and places in Cuba which may be in the actual possession of our land and naval forces will be opened to the commerce of all neutral nations, as well as our own, in articles not contraband of war, upon payment of the prescribed rates of duty which may be in force at the time of the importation.

WILLIAM McKINLEY.

By order of the Secretary of War:

H. C. CORBIN, Adjutant General.

www.ingramcontent.com/pod-product-compliance
Lightning Source LLC
Chambersburg PA
CBHW021524090426
42739CB00007B/764